T0228792

A gift for

_____

From

_____

Date

_____

REVIVE

DECLARATIONS OF
GOD'S TRUTH
TO RENEW YOUR SPIRIT

CLEERE CHERRY REAVES

THOMAS NELSON
Since 1798

Published in Nashville, Tennessee, by Thomas Nelson. Thomas Nelson is a registered trademark of HarperCollins Christian Publishing, Inc.

Published in association with the literary agency of Wolgemuth & Wilson.

Thomas Nelson titles may be purchased in bulk for educational, business, fund-raising, or sales promotional use. For information, please email SpecialMarkets@ThomasNelson.com.

Unless otherwise noted, Scripture quotations are from the Holy Bible, New International Version®, NIV®. Copyright © 1973, 1978, 1984, 2011 by Biblica, Inc.® Used by permission of Zondervan. All rights reserved worldwide. www.zondervan.com. The "NIV" and "New International Version" are trademarks registered in the United States Patent and Trademark Office by Biblica, Inc.®

Scripture quotations marked BSB are from the Holy Bible, Berean Study Bible, BSB. Copyright © 2016, 2018 by Bible Hub. Used by permission. All rights reserved worldwide.

Scripture quotations marked ESV are from the ESV® Bible (The Holy Bible, English Standard Version®). Copyright © 2001 by Crossway, a publishing ministry of Good News Publishers. Used by permission. All rights reserved.

Scripture quotations marked NASB are from the New American Standard Bible® (NASB). Copyright © 1960, 1962, 1963, 1968, 1971, 1972, 1973, 1975, 1977, 1995, 2020 by The Lockman Foundation. Used by permission. www.Lockman.org.

Scripture quotations marked NKJV are from the New King James Version®. Copyright © 1982 by Thomas Nelson. Used by permission. All rights reserved.

Scripture quotations marked NLT are from the Holy Bible, New Living Translation. Copyright © 1996, 2004, 2015 by Tyndale House Foundation. Used by permission of Tyndale House Ministries, Carol Stream, Illinois 60188. All rights reserved.

Any internet addresses, phone numbers, or company or product information printed in this book are offered as a resource and are not intended in any way to be or to imply an endorsement by Thomas Nelson, nor does Thomas Nelson vouch for the existence, content, or services of these sites, phone numbers, companies, or products beyond the life of this book.

ISBN 978-1-4002-4219-1 (HC)
ISBN 978-1-4002-4222-1 (audiobook)
ISBN 978-1-4002-4220-7 (eBook)

Printed in Malaysia

24 25 26 27 28 OFF 10 9 8 7 6 5 4 3 2 1

Contents

Contents

To my family and friends who encouraged me to keep writing, even when I felt like nobody was listening. I am forever grateful for you. The way you show up in the world inspires me to keep showing up and trusting God with the outcome. I pray this book reminds you that nothing is too dry or dead for God to revive it.

You are loved,
Cleere

Introduction

Hi, friend!

First, I want to say thank you. Thank you for picking up this book, thank you for believing that God has something to say to you, and thank you for being intentional with your life. I am really proud of you. Since I can't have a one-on-one conversation with every reader, my prayer is always that you feel the warmth and power of the Holy Spirit through every word. I hope that you learn more about the depth of the love Jesus has for you and that your life would be a reflection of it.

This devotional is different from the other books I have written; I believe the format is uniquely set up to help head knowledge become heart knowledge. Each week includes a main scripture to meditate on, a devotion to help you think through that particular theme or topic in your life, and five declarations to apply for the week ahead. I have found that identifying and voicing healthy, specific rhythms provide a strong foundation and clear intentions for our lives. I have personally written out weekly declarations for myself and my family for several years now, and in doing so, I have learned the importance of using centralized, personal, and specific key points that provide grounding application to walk out our faith.

I genuinely believe that if you are intentional with this book and practice these declarations, God will use it to work miracles inside you, through you, and around you. When you meditate on the character of God and let that determine your perspective, everything shifts, even if nothing around you changes.

My hope is that the pages of this book will look weathered and worn because you have rehearsed these words in your car, in your living room, in your office, or wherever you find yourself sitting with Jesus. How would your life change if you trusted God to be exactly who He says He is? Where would you go or stay? How would you travel? What would your words sound like?

When I think about what kind of person I long to be, it's a person of peace. I yearn to be someone who walks with the assurance of heaven at the forefront of my mind at all times. Approaching life circumstances from a place of fulfillment and safety is the richest kind of life. I pray that I don't just talk about the life-changing power of the Holy Spirit, but I let Him infuse every fiber of my being and direct every part of my life. Don't you want that?

The abundant life where strength, refreshment, and hope are in unlimited supply is available to you and to me. Let's let Jesus revive us, not withholding a single area of our hearts, trusting that His truth really can quench our thirst.

Grab a friend, walk through this with your family, or work through it with Jesus in your time together.

Whatever you do, don't let this be just another book that you check off your list. Plant your life in His promises and cling to what is true.

Cheering you on and grateful for your life!

Love,

Cleere

1

Trust Him with Open and Closed Doors

I t didn't make sense to me. God was telling me no, but it seemed like He was telling everyone else yes. I thought I was ready for the promotion I'd prayed for at work, but it turns out God had something else for me. What I originally interpreted as rejection became the provision for me to work smarter, dig deeper into the strategic side of the business, and hone my focus. I later received a promotion that was much better suited to my gifts, personality, and skill set. But without the "not yet" packaged as a "no," that door would have never opened.

I've discovered that many of the answered prayers I am most thankful for are the ones to which God said no or not yet. The circumstances that felt like closed doors at the time were, in fact, the hallway to the open door I didn't know I was searching for.

Sometimes it's hard to remember there is so much we don't know and so little we can see from our finite point of view. This is especially true when we feel like we've been wandering in the wilderness for longer than we'd hoped, or that our prayers are falling on deaf ears. God is not surprised by the fear that uncertainty can bring to our days. When a job promotion doesn't happen, when financial stress looms large, when a relationship seems too hard, or when a season of struggle seems to linger too long, lean into the infallible Word of God. Ask the Holy Spirit to help you personalize it right where you are. His Word meets you in the thick of every situation—both the hard and the happy. It also helps you remember that He's equipped you not just to survive this season but to thrive in every season.

Here is a certainty you can stand on this week: every open and closed door is a gift when the Shepherd is leading you. As you enter His presence, invite a spirit of calm and remind your soul of this truth, even when it feels hard to believe: God is using every open and closed door for your ultimate good. Not a short-term, shortsighted version of good but an everlasting, ever-present, undeniably beautiful kind of good—the kind of good you crave. That is what He has for you this week. Will you trust Him with it?

DECLARE OVER YOUR WEEK:

1. I will believe that God is working all things for my good and His glory by opening and closing doors.

2. I will put on the full armor of God every day.

3. I will read the Word and lean into the Spirit for the true definition of *good*.

4. I will ask for joy, hope, and peace when I need them—confident that Jesus hears me and He will provide.

5. I will praise God for the week ahead, knowing He is in control and He always operates in love.

2

The Power of Constant Conversation

Waking up, I offer, "Hey, Jesus, good morning. Thank You for this day! Will You help me see it with fresh eyes? Give me new vision." Several hours later, I report, "Me again, headed into lunch with a friend. Will You guide this conversation? Thank You for this time." Later, I celebrate, "Thank You for that moment, Jesus! You connected those dots before I even realized they were related!" Soon after, I beg, "Lord, what would You do in this situation? Guide me here." All day, in every space, amid whatever struggle, asking any questions, I invite God to join me where I am.

If you truly believed that the King of the universe, the Controller and Knower of all things, was listening to your prayers and cared about your heart, do you think you would pray more? When life feels nerve-racking or the world feels scary, wouldn't prayer become your greatest strategy?

The hard truth about our prayer life is getting honest about why prayer is not our first response. It is not because we lack the time, need fancier words, or aren't spiritual enough. It's because we forget who we're praying to—and that He's actually listening. The Bible shares miracle after miracle of when God's people stopped relying on their own strength and turned to prayer. This same God who hears your prayers is the One who calmed the seas. He's the One who made the sun stand still and performed seemingly impossible miracles. *That's* who you have direct access to at every moment.

Prayer delights God, but His instruction for you to pray continually is for your own benefit—because He knows that prayer is the surest way to safety, the quickest pathway to peace, and the richest rhythm you can establish in your life. Prayer is His protection and provision over you.

This week, as you begin your day, pray. When you have a conversation, pray. As you walk into new spaces, pray. While you work, pray. Before you make a decision, pray. Communicate with Jesus, and you will find the clarity, courage, and confidence you're craving.

No matter what this week holds, He's given you all that you need to be recharged, renewed, and refreshed. Will you connect with Him before everything?

DECLARE OVER YOUR WEEK:

1. I will devote myself to bring everything to the Father, knowing that nothing is too big or too small for Him. I will commit to being my full self before God.

2. I will unplug whenever possible, allowing moments for my soul to be recharged, renewed, and refreshed.

3. I will believe in the power and effectiveness of prayer.

4. I will talk to Jesus and ask Him to help me see others through His eyes of compassion and gentleness.

5. I will model my prayer life after Jesus, who prayed intentionally, passionately, and continually to His Father in heaven.

3

Abiding Under His Wings

orn three months early, he weighed only one pound. After our conversation with the doctor, we knew that our stint in the hospital would not be a short one. As a new mama navigating a sterile world that felt anything but normal, I knew that if I didn't attach myself to the Vine—and remain completely intertwined with Him and His Word—I wouldn't have what it took to travel the journey well. Without God's warmth, strength, and peace amid a journey weighted with uncertainty and hardship, I would have withered away.

While it doesn't always feel like it, the truth is, your need is actually the richest thing about you. It is the very thing that invites the power of the Holy Spirit to work within you, and for God to be known by the world around you. It forces you to surrender your pride and go to the feet of the One who made you, and ask, "God, can You help me? Can You provide what I cannot?"

This week, be vulnerable with Jesus about what weighs heavy on your mind or what you're wrestling with. He loves when you voice what you need, even when you feel like you just asked for more yesterday. It is so comforting to know that we cannot exhaust His patience.

God knows what you're facing today. Whether your health diagnosis is uncertain, your finances seem shaky, your emotions are overwhelming, your family is dysfunctional, or your future feels fearful, remember who your Shepherd is. The same God who split apart the sea and made ways in the wilderness is watching over you. The space between your comfort zone and where God is calling you is the exact place where faith resides and trust thrives—where you get to be a doer of the Word and live out your belief. When you walk in courage even in the uncomfortable, Jesus is glorified.

The best part is, the more you realize the depth of your need, the greater you experience His love: unmatched, unconditional, and unwavering. As you hide yourself in Him, He will help you make your heart His home, which then leads to a stable, loving, and joyful place for those you love. What a blessing.

Remember, your need is your superpower. Lean into it, not away from it.

DECLARE OVER YOUR WEEK:

1. Instead of resisting my needs, I will notice them and seek what I need in God.

2. I will trust God's covering over my health, my finances, my emotions, my family, and my future.

3. I will live a life that reflects the truth I know and trust.

4. I will keep my "why" at the forefront of my mind and let it fuel my steps.

5. I will seek to create a stable, loving, and joyful home and heart.

4

The Security to Step Out of the Boat

My SUV was packed to the brim. I'd said my goodbyes, and there was no turning back. I was moving to Texas from North Carolina and the anticipation in my heart was palpable. Though I was leaving the familiar, I had never felt more certain that this big change was right because I was following the way of peace. I was planting new roots, fully expectant of what God was going to do. In that moment, stepping out of the boat onto unknown waters felt like the safest thing I could do. Years later, I still try to remember this when the way forward doesn't seem so obvious, or the peace feels a little harder to find.

Wouldn't it be nice to see the entire map of our journey before leaving the shoreline so we'd know there is purpose and provision ahead? But if that were the case, would we even need faith?

This week, you will have many opportunities to step out of the boat and onto the seas. Where you fix your eyes will determine whether you take part in miracles or draw back out of fear. When something unexpected happens and anxiety begins to swirl, or when the timing of events in your life feels unfair or too hard, it's tempting to fix your eyes too low. Your phone might be a tempting place to land. Friends may seem immediately available, social media might offer a quick dopamine fix, and distractions might numb the pain for a little while. But remember, you have direct access to and the undivided attention of the Maker of the seas. He will never take His eyes off you.

Your life was never meant to be a story of mere survival as you stay safely in the harbor; rather, you have the opportunity to walk in courage as the Waymaker reminds you that He is the only Comforter you need. Step forward, knowing only the next step He has revealed to you and trusting that His authority is sovereign, His care is top-notch, and He knows the end from the beginning. You don't need to know the whole picture, just the Promise-Keeper.

It turns out that the unknowns and detours can become your favorite parts of your story, reminding you that nearness to the Author of life is the point behind it all. You don't have to figure out your future; you just have to figure out who you trust with your future.

Get excited—the pressure is off, and miracles are on the horizon! Your future is secure because there is no safer place than in your Father's grasp.

DECLARE OVER YOUR WEEK:

1. I will be intentional about stepping outside my comfort zone as often as possible. That's where faith lives.

2. I will bring my anxieties, doubts, and fears to God's feet before retreating to my phone.

3. I will pray for miracles over my life and the lives of those around me.

4. I will stop striving for God and let my focus be enjoying God.

5. I will get excited as I anticipate His work in my life.

5

Calmed by the Counselor

Whoever is slow to anger is better than the mighty,
and he who rules his spirit than he who takes a city.

PROVERBS 16:32 ESV

I knew they weren't trying to exclude me. But my heart was struggling. My friends had planned an excursion but hadn't mentioned it to me. My heart sank as I was transported back to middle school, feeling the deep pain of rejection. I knew the hurt would become a bigger deal than it needed to be if I didn't take it to God. And as I sat and sorted it out with Jesus, I was reminded of my value. He even helped me recalibrate by offering a different perspective that allowed me to let go of the offense.

We often focus too much on our emotions, letting them steer us and inform our decisions. Or sometimes we focus too little on our emotions, which causes us to suppress or avoid reality, further holding us back from where we want to go.

Your emotions are not a burden to God. Think about this: He made you. He made your heart, He made your mind, and He made your soul. Reading through the book of Psalms, we see that David voiced a million different emotions: anguish, anger, joy, gratitude, anxiety, anticipation. Let this be a reminder that Jesus is a safe place to sort through anything you feel, big or small. He doesn't find you too much or not enough, but He does long for your emotions to be indicators, not dictators, of your thoughts, decisions, and actions moving forward.

This week, there will be times when you will be saddened by the world around you, frustrated by traffic or kids or work. There will be other moments when you're jubilant about new growth or an answered prayer. No matter the emotion, go to Jesus with each of them. You magnify God with your life when you invite Him to be the Lord of every part of it. His greatest delight is when you invite Him into every space. Don't forget: He died for every part of you.

The sooner you take your emotions to Him, the quicker you will be able to filter what is true, and the more you will be able to offer grace to yourself and those around you. You will never regret bringing your emotions into His presence.

Feel what you feel, and then ask Jesus what's real and how to deal. He will help you.

DECLARE OVER YOUR WEEK:

1. I will communicate with Jesus, sharing every emotion with Him.

2. I will remember the consistency of every sunrise.

3. I will magnify God with my whole life, committing every area to Him.

4. Because I don't have to hide anything from the One who knows it all, I will welcome the light in every situation.

5. I will walk bravely into my future, fully trusting Jesus to meet me there.

6

The Stones in Your Pocket

Reaching into his shepherd's bag and taking out a stone, he hurled it with his sling and hit the Philistine in the forehead. The stone sank in, and Goliath stumbled and fell face down on the ground.

1 SAMUEL 17:49 NLT

Confrontation has never been my strong suit. My throat tightens and my stomach tangles into a million knots. Once, when anticipating a hard conversation, I had prayed often. As my friend and I sat down and began to speak, it was obvious that somehow, some way, God had softened her heart. By the time we finished, though our disagreement wasn't tied up neatly with a bow, we both knew that healing had begun. And as we parted ways, I felt Jesus smile at my willingness to show up despite the pain.

Can you remember situations when you felt ill-equipped to handle what was in front of you, but later you realized God was making a way?

Only God knows what we're capable of doing with Him by our side. Just like we see throughout the Bible and in testimonies all around us, when the favor of God is on our life, nothing and no one can stand in our way.

This week, as you enter conversations, engage with others, and encounter circumstances that feel heavy or hard, remember God's provision to ensure your victory against every giant. Go back to the story of David and Goliath. David didn't see Goliath as the unbeatable, unmatched warrior that everyone else did; he saw Goliath as the person on the other side of God's unstoppable strength. The stones in his pocket turned from power-less to purposeful because he walked in the confidence of the Lord.

Let go of where you thought you would be or how you thought your life would look and embrace the place you are right now. Ask God to show you how He has pre-pared you for this season and reflect on His favor over your past. Flip your perspective from "Oh no, there are giants ahead!" to "I get to take part in defeating giants!" As you walk in confidence because of His provision, declare vic-tory and discover the God-sized destiny He has for your life. Because the Holy Spirit lives in you, you have influ-ence. Because the Holy Spirit lives in you, you have the fruit of the Spirit at your constant disposal. When you feel frustrated, remember your patience. Trust the goodness of God when He tells you that His plans for you are good, and choose to walk in peace no matter what others say.

Be a David on the battlefield of your life this week. Survey the stones in your pocket, walk forward in trust, and be an example to everyone watching.

DECLARE OVER YOUR WEEK:

1. I will trust that God has equipped me to face any Goliath in my way this week.

2. I will realize the influence I have where I am and take it seriously.

3. I will walk forward, remembering that the favor of God is upon my life. He is for me.

4. I will let go of what I thought would happen and lean into what God is doing right now.

5. I will choose patience over frustration, celebration over jealousy, belief over doubt, and peace over worry.

7

The Friend I Can Always Count On

While Jesus was here on earth, he offered prayers and pleadings, with a loud cry and tears, to the one who could rescue him from death. And God heard his prayers because of his deep reverence for God.

HEBREWS 5:7 NLT

Have you ever had the experience of connecting with someone in such a powerful way that you chat about anything and everything for hours on end?

Who do you spend the most time talking to? Maybe it's your spouse, your parents, your best friend, or your children. Think about those conversations—do their countenance, responses, and advice affect how you handle your day or impact your mood? Now consider this: How often do you talk to Jesus, tell Him about your daily happenings, and ask Him for His advice on how to handle the little and big parts of your day?

Sometimes when we think of talking to Jesus as "prayer," it feels like there should be a level of formality or maybe a formula to follow. This can make us feel like Jesus is far away—like He is busy or unaware, or like He doesn't have relevant insight for us. But what if this week you talked to Him as you're heading to a meeting, driving in the car, or navigating the barrage of emotions that find their way into your day? What do you think this open dialogue would change?

You have the incredible opportunity to speak to Jesus every step of the way. Choose to bring all of you—the broken, the beautiful, the "but I'm still working on it" parts—and give it to Him. Receive His favor and ask for His guidance over every portion of your life. Surrendering your all keeps the Enemy from getting a foothold in any space.

When you're feeling happy and on top of the world, talk to Jesus about His kindness. When you're feeling insecure about your gifts, talk to Jesus about His sovereignty and purpose over everything He makes. When you're feeling frustrated by family, impatient at work, or discouraged by people in general, ask Jesus to help you see His goodness in every place and every person. You never need to feel alone in your emotions. Your Creator wants to hear about them—all of them—and He promises to help you address and move through them without shame. How powerful is that?

Let your heart take in His wonder, and worship Him with your words—it will change your life.

DECLARE OVER YOUR WEEK:

1. I will talk to Jesus about all the things, all week long.

2. I will invite Him into the seen and unseen places, letting Him permeate every place in my life.

3. I will speak life into my relationships, recognizing the strengths of those around me.

4. I will meditate on His Word and sort through any doubts I have with the One who is the living Word.

5. I will let the truth that Jesus loves me lead and light every word I say and every step I take.

8

Pressure Removed; Peace Gained

My heart was breaking. How could this hurt so much when I knew it was the right decision? I had to leave a relationship that left me wondering why God couldn't just fix the broken pieces rather than ask me to end it. Finally, after endless tears, I did my best to surrender it to Him. And still, I had to lay it down countless more times. But every time I did, the hurt and the weight became a little lighter.

Think about the times you decided to give your burdens to Jesus and leave them at His feet. Have you ever regretted it? Has there ever been a time when you have put the pressure back on God's shoulders, and He has let you down?

Even when things feel uncertain and life doesn't resemble the picture we've created in our minds, there is something so freeing about knowing the burdens are no longer in our hands but in our Savior's. This allows our minds to take a breather from the overwhelming details of life. The problems that once felt so loud and mighty begin to shrink in comparison to the size of our God. The strained and difficult relationships in our lives become reminders of our dependence on the One who has made every heart and soul. He is aware of the circumstances, He understands the tension, and He is the One who can soften any heart. The unexpected hardships that feel confusing and the harrowing challenges that feel impossible to overcome? They remind us that God holds every single one in His hand. Nothing is too hard for Him.

And this is where we will find peace.

You see, peace is not the result of everything coming together perfectly and your plan unfolding exactly as you dreamed. Peace is the result of trusting that the only perfect One is holding everything together, and His plans are greater than you could ever imagine. Take the leap of faith and walk forward in obedience, even if your feet are shaking and your heart is clinging in full force to the Shepherd.

Assess the load you're carrying into this week—what can stay, and what needs to go? Don't you feel lighter when you realize that you've been set free from living from a place of fear, scarcity, or stress? Peace can be your posture because the presence of Jesus is always with you.

DECLARE OVER YOUR WEEK:

1. I will give Jesus my burdens.

2. I will ask God to help me see my circumstances from heaven's point of view.

3. I will trust that I have been equipped with unique gifts for the place the Lord has brought me.

4. When I am fearful, I will keep taking steps of faith.

5. I will settle my soul in the unchanging love and unshakable peace of God.

9

He's as
Close as
Your Breath

My friend mused, "The only way He could have known to help me in this way is if His eyes had never left me." As I watched this friend sort out how God had redeemed a tragedy in his life and turned it into a time of transformation and strength, I was deeply encouraged. For years, the Holy Spirit had felt distant and confusing to him. But now the Spirit was the One he was hearing from and trusting.

When you think about the Holy Spirit, do you think of Him as your personal companion, or does He seem distant or difficult to understand?

When Jesus was preparing to take up the cross and go to heaven, He gave His followers the gift of the Holy Spirit. In fact, He said that He had to go so that Someone better could come alongside us and live within us. Jesus did not take all His power with Him; He multiplied it and provided it to you in the person of the Holy Spirit. However, so many people in the church operate with a vague understanding of Him. They're hesitant to let Him in or accept Him as a friend. Sometimes this comes from a lack of understanding, a misinterpretation of how personal He is, or a fear of what surrender might require of them. Where do you fall in this spectrum of understanding?

The week ahead of you will contain many turns and unexpected pivots. It is the Holy Spirit who provides the wisdom to know which way to go, the discernment to know what to bring, and the courage to keep walking forward. Allow the Holy Spirit to be your constant companion. He is a gift from the Father. However, it is up to you to walk in the power that He offers.

As you receive His strength and reacquaint yourself with His love, reprioritize your schedule in accordance with where He is guiding you. You don't have to worry about what may fall; His will and grace protect what you can't cover. This week, expect the revival of the Holy Spirit to bring new health to your home and heart as you let His hope become your North Star.

A restful life is one where the Holy Spirit resides. How wonderful to know He is with you always.

DECLARE OVER YOUR WEEK:

1. I will ask the Holy Spirit to help me redefine my perspective in every space.

2. I will trust that I have been prepared for whatever I will face in the week ahead.

3. I will surrender my plans and let the Spirit reprioritize according to His order and design.

4. I will anticipate the revival that the Holy Spirit will bring in my home, in my relationships, and in my everyday interactions.

5. I will rest in knowing He has readied, redefined, reprioritized, and revived my spirit.

The
Discipline
of Being
Present

As I gazed at the mountains in the distance, the cool breeze swirled around me, and I cupped my warm coffee in hand. I was embracing the quiet for the first time in a while. But as I tried to dig into the scriptures I was reading, the most random worry invaded my mind: *What if I suddenly lose my creativity?* Here I was in the most serene place to practice solitude, surrounded by the painted landscape of the Creator Himself, and I was worrying about whether I would lose the very gift He gave me.

Have you ever noticed how your mind can travel a million miles in just a few minutes? Even when you're trying to practice solitude, it seems that you have a bundle of tabs open in your head, and tackling them all feels impossible. I call it "squirreling out"—when your mind feels scattered and isn't able to focus on the current task, journey, or conversation at hand. Have you experienced this all-too-familiar phenomenon?

There is a reason why Jesus, the only perfect One, continually made time to sit still with the Father and reflect on His faithfulness. Jesus set aside time in His schedule to receive His Father's affection and renew Himself in truth. Why? Because He knew that for His mind to stay focused and calm, He had to slow His pace and ask the Spirit to help Him be present. Don't you think that means you can benefit from doing the same?

The Enemy can't steal your destiny or rewrite your identity, so he will do everything he can to distract you. He will try to discourage you in the present by making you obsess over the future, knowing you can't do anything about tomorrow. Reserve your energy for *this* moment, *this* day, *this* season. And this week, you will make decisions that have long-term impacts. During this time, ask yourself, *Do I trust God with tomorrow?*

Day by day, be diligent about practicing awareness, solitude, and prayer. Being present is a discipline that requires practice, so be gentle with yourself. Understand that while it's normal to occasionally obsess over the past or feel paralyzed by the future, you have the Holy Spirit to help you remain in the present, fully committed to exactly what God has planned for this day.

Make today great and know that you can trust Him with every tomorrow.

DECLARE OVER YOUR WEEK:

1. I will pay attention to what is in front of me this day.

2. I will sit with Jesus every morning, even for a few moments, and soak in His love.

3. I will pay attention to the fuel in my tank, realizing when I need to persevere and when I need to take a break.

4. My emotional equilibrium will not be determined by what happened in the past or my worries about the future.

5. I will lean on the power of prayer, understanding that the One listening controls heaven and earth.

11

When Grace Determines Your Posture

> "I have swept away your offenses like a cloud, your sins like the morning mist. Return to me, for I have redeemed you."
>
> **ISAIAH 44:22**

I magine a scene where a couple is getting ready for the day when the woman notices that her husband has shrunk her favorite shirt. She has two choices: She can get upset at his carelessness and let it start her off in a bad mood. Or she can extend grace, realize he was trying to be helpful, and decide not to let this small thing steal her joy. Though this seems like a trivial example, it is the little moments where we decide to embrace grace and see God work that provide the framework to maintain a posture of grace when it's something much bigger.

Do you see how the response she chooses will determine her experience?

We hear about grace, talk about grace, and sing about grace. We know it's the foundation for the faith we have. However, there is a big difference in knowing *about* grace and letting it determine the way we think and act. When we catch even a tiny glimpse of the redemption we have received, it gives us the strength and hope to show up fully in our lives, no matter how hard-pressed we may feel or how high the odds may be stacked against us. When we see life through our Savior's eyes, we recognize His favor over our past and present, and we gain confidence over His hold on our future.

This week, remember that you don't have to earn the love of the One who died to save you. Remember that each moment is an opportunity to do good, not because you are attempting to earn His affirmation, but because you are already walking in the adoration of the King. Direct your energy toward abiding in His arms and delighting in His strength. He is a God of restoration, bringing life to dry places and hope to weary hearts—that is His specialty! How comforting to know that all suffering is short-lived and that you can experience His healing power firsthand. After all, how would you know to trust His safety net if you never had to fall into it?

Whether you have a relationship that is struggling, a work situation that feels beyond repair, a bank account that keeps you up at night, or a problem you just can't seem to shake, go back to the foundation of grace. Let your posture be one of responding to heaven's view, not reacting to earth's circumstances. If God says it's so, then it is so. As sure as the sunrise, it is so. Hold tightly to every word He says.

DECLARE OVER YOUR WEEK:

1. I will find safety, strength, and security in the arms of Jesus.

2. I will do good, not because I am trying to earn God's favor but because God is always faithful.

3. Reclaiming any area in which I've let the Enemy have a voice, I trust the Holy Spirit will help me take back my ground with authority, faith, and peace.

4. I will trust that if God says it's so, then it is so.

5. I will view rain clouds as opportunities to have a front-row seat to witness His rainbow.

12

The Secret Weapon of Humility

But he gives us more grace. That is why
Scripture says: "God opposes the proud
but shows favor to the humble."

JAMES 4:6

My pride flared up as I saw the reply to my text. When the words arrived, I protested inside, thinking, *That is* not *what happened!* I knew I was in the right and began to wonder how I would defend myself. I was feeling gaslighted, my offense was increasing by the second, and my pride bullied me: *People will believe her if you don't set them straight.* Deep in my spirit, though, I knew that proving I was right wasn't worth it. Choosing to walk with integrity, I decided that the Holy Spirit would be my advocate.

Have you ever regretted surrendering your pride? Really, take a moment to consider this. Whether it involved a conversation with a friend, a decision you've made, or forgiveness you've extended, have you ever walked with humility and wished you hadn't?

It is easy to talk about humility and the difference it makes, until we're on the receiving end of an offense or desperately want to prove that we're right. Suddenly humility no longer seems like a fun virtue to extend; pride and spite seem a lot easier to dish out in the moment. But humility paves the path to holiness, because it is often the hard, countercultural choice to put God's way over ours. It's hard because it means prioritizing the values and views of heaven over the validation of the world. It's hard because it requires relinquishing our pride and choosing to trust that the heavenly Father's protection over us is sufficient.

Humility is your secret weapon, helping you gain perspective and tap into His supernatural power as you seek His presence. So choose to sit at your Father's table before inviting people to your own. Doing so will equip you with the ability to extend kindness, offer warmth, and give love that wasn't accessible before.

This week, don't be surprised when your flesh wants to be recognized. Take this as an indicator to slow down and talk to the Holy Spirit. Listen as He calls you back into His embrace, whispering, *Rest with Me awhile.* Choose to sit with the Shepherd, and you will receive the strength and sustenance your heart is craving.

What an honor you have this week—to begin again with Jesus, to humble yourself at His feet, and to extend that heart of acceptance to a broken world so hungry for the real thing. The knee prints formed by a humble soul will always make an impression on the prideful world around it.

DECLARE OVER YOUR WEEK:

1. I will release my pride, trusting the Holy Spirit to be my defender.

2. I will work hard, offering an attitude of excellence and a posture of humility no matter the recognition I receive.

3. I will invite others to my table, offering warmth, acceptance, and love no matter who they are or what they have.

4. I will pay attention to the nudges of the Holy Spirit, trusting that where He leads is the pathway to wisdom and grace.

5. I will choose to prioritize the values and views of heaven over the voices and validation of the world.

Choosing Self-Control When It's Not Easy

Like a city whose walls are broken through
is a person who lacks self-control.
PROVERBS 25:28

I was exhausted after preparing for a big presentation for work. Frustrated by the fact that my colleagues had delegated the bulk of the project to me, I wanted to stop short and teach them a lesson. However, I knew that by doing that I would hurt myself as well. Though I stayed the course, I remember having to really fight my flesh. I had to remind myself that the person I was representing was Jesus—not myself. That helped me to practice self-control.

Have you ever struggled to do what you know is best for you? Most of the good things that come to us— family relationships, a healthy church community, positive mental and physical health—require slow and steady commitment. What do you do when you find yourself tempted to slack off or veer from what you know is best?

It doesn't feel glamorous to talk about self-control, does it? It doesn't sound fun or exciting, but the reality of your week is this: your peace and your power will be based on your ability to walk in self-control. The things you say yes and no to will determine the road you travel and the destiny you experience.

There will never be a shortage of distractions or alluring opportunities that offer immediate gratification. That's why Jesus talked about self-control throughout Scripture; He won't be surprised when you want to turn down roads that aren't for you. That's why He reminds you that you've been equipped to endure, powered to persevere, and set apart to be self-disciplined in the Spirit.

The Creator wired your body, wove your heart together, and has written your story, so you don't have to fear the future. If you're living according to God's Word, you're right where you need to be. Remember who is for you, who is with you, and who lives inside you. It is impossible for the Keeper of your soul to take you down a path that is bad for you.

What practices help you stay focused on God when you feel tempted? Craft rhythms around those disciplines. What guards your mind from things to avoid and opens your heart to pay attention to life-giving truths? Self-control is a muscle, strengthened by walking in awareness in the smallest of ways.

Let the calming presence of the Holy Spirit set the tone for each day. Self-control is your companion because the Holy Spirit is your Helper.

DECLARE OVER YOUR WEEK:

1. I will practice self-control in my thought life.

2. I will proclaim truth and hope over every area of my life.

3. I will keep my eyes on things that uplift my soul and support my peace.

4. I will trust the Good Shepherd to meet my every emotional, physical, mental, and spiritual need.

5. I will be slow to jump to conclusions, letting the calming presence of the Holy Spirit guide my mind and heart.

14

Be a Safe Place of Refuge

And thus you shall greet him: "Peace
be to you, and peace be to your house,
and peace be to all that you have."

1 SAMUEL 25:6 ESV

efuge. In the home-building process I've been navigating the past year, I have repeatedly said to my builder, "I want my home to feel like a refuge to all who enter." It's what I hope my home operates as, smells like, sleeps like, tastes like, and feels like to everyone. No matter who you are, where you come from, what you bring, or how you arrive, I pray that my home is always a place of safety, security, and strength. Psalm 91 promises that all will find refuge under God's wings, and I pray people receive a small taste of that comfort and peace within the walls of the space we've built.

If you had a banner over your home, what would you like it to say? What legacy do you want your family to leave behind? What do you hope your family represents to the watching world?

The banner over anyplace you enter sets the tone and establishes expectations. We could also call it a "mission statement." And nothing is more important than deciding the mission statement within the walls of your home, because the way you live in private determines how you see, respond, and understand the world outside those walls.

As you go into your community this week, you'll choose whether to walk in the way of the world or stand firm in the way of the Word. Every decision and every conversation will provide opportunities to practice being who God has called you to be. Do not be surprised when it seems more romantic or exciting to follow the ways of the world. When these moments arrive, remember the banner you've declared over your home and the legacy you've been writing with your life. And remember you're not the only one who's been working here. Before the physical walls of your home ever came to be, the Builder of your heart spoke identity, truth, and worth over you and your family.

Let the threshold of your home be a place where others experience the kindness and grace of God. Pray for opportunities to let others into your refuge, and look for simple ways that your walls may be a blessing to others. Expect miracles to take place in your home as you depend on Jesus to lead your thoughts, words, actions, choices, and legacy. *That's* your banner.

Refuge is what your home gets to be.

Refreshment is what your home gets to offer.

Revival is what the Spirit will provide in your heart and your home if you let Him.

DECLARE OVER YOUR WEEK:

1. My home will be a place of praise, kindness, healing, and grace.

2. I will order my week with diligence and preparation while remaining adaptable and patient.

3. I will yield to my Father's instruction, no matter what He asks.

4. In deep waters, I will tighten my grip on His hand and trust His provision.

5. I will invite the One who doesn't slumber to watch over me as I sleep.

Dream with the Hope Giver

F or a while, I thought I had forgotten how to dream. Not nighttime dreams, but the inspirational kind of vision that lives in our hearts. In the very depths of my soul, I genuinely was afraid that maybe I had stopped dreaming. Then, in the middle of a random conversation, I felt the Holy Spirit whisper, *This is a dream realized.* I didn't even recognize it until I took a step back and noticed what God was doing in that interaction. When I felt like I couldn't dream, the great Helper was still sowing seeds and watering desires. It was wildly comforting to know that He was doing what I could not.

When is the last time you let your heart dream aloud with the Father?

Sometimes, as we get older and gain more responsibility, we forget what it looks like to nourish the dreams in our heart. We become so used to stuffing them down because they feel unrealistic or uncertain. Or maybe we allow ourselves to take a few leaps of faith and then the stress of the unknown feels too overwhelming. At that point, we're tempted to stay stagnant, shrink back, or sulk in worry about the future. But Jesus—the One who birthed those dreams and propels every good and holy thing forward—has a different way.

This week, decide to live with your eyes wide open and your hands fully available to what the Promise-Keeper has in store. Don't let the weight of the unknown drown out your excitement for what God has in store for you. Travel lightly and freely. Use the tools He has given you and watch as your dreams come to fruition.

You are a city on a hill, a light that is meant to shine for all the world to see. Don't hide your light; the world around you desperately needs it. This week is brand-new, full of fresh grace, new mercy, and a million chances to show up and try again.

Let your heart dream with the One who wove it together. Give all that you have and then rest, knowing that rest is given by the Redeemer Himself. Isn't that wildly comforting? You get to choose courage and trust, knowing that He will always choose consistency, faithfulness, and love in return.

DECLARE OVER YOUR WEEK:

1. I will dream together with God, letting His supernatural energy infuse me with passion.

2. I will trust that every new horizon brings fresh grace and new mercy.

3. I will utilize my gifts, walk in my strengths, and be honest about the dreams on my heart.

4. I will be quick to take my stress to the Shepherd, letting worship replace my overwhelm as truth relaxes my soul.

5. My focus will be on the Promise-Keeper. I can trust His ways.

God-Confidence > Self-Confidence

Some days we may feel exhausted, struggling to enjoy what we used to love. We find ourselves trying to please those around us and don't take care of ourselves at all. Other days, we may be more focused on us. Maybe serving others feels inconvenient. Perhaps we're easily offended. Both ways of being leave us unfulfilled: neglecting ourselves and feeling empty or being consumed by ourselves and . . . also feeling empty.

There tend to be two extremes in how we treat ourselves: either we operate in total self-sabotage and assume it's selfish to care for our own souls, or we hyperfocus on ourselves and become completely consumed in our own bubbles. Both leave us dissatisfied. So where is the middle ground?

Our souls crave God-confidence. The kind of confidence that infuses us with energy, trusting God's truths about who we are and not fixating on getting attention from the world around us. The kind of confidence that allows us to take our energy outward to do good to others, rather than focusing on how others perceive us.

This week, choose to be kind, reliable, and gracious

to yourself. Not because you won't mess up, but rather because you will—and Jesus will still claim you, want to use you, and speak promises over your every step. When you mess up, don't let yourself wallow in your sin for longer than you need to. Believe that God is ready to forgive and ask Him to direct your steps to get back on mission. Let your God-given identity direct your day, offering you peace and strength in every hour.

Don't be surprised when others don't understand your mission or the timeline doesn't line up with what culture says is acceptable. You have the power of the Holy Spirit inside you—that means the living God has decided to take up residence in your heart and equip you with the creativity, courage, and capability that only heaven can provide. When you give God your best and let His confidence become the foundation of your life, you will thrive.

Draw a circle around yourself—this is the only person you can control. Dig deep into the love of the Father. Refuse to live in self-obsession and decide that this week you will saturate everything you do in the unmerited favor of the living God. Let His love be your confidence.

DECLARE OVER YOUR WEEK:

1. I will wake up each day and walk in God-confidence.

2. I will be a kind and reliable friend to myself, encouraging my own heart and believing God's truth about myself.

3. I will walk in the assurance of God's timeline, not letting the pressure from the world cripple my perspective or confidence.

4. I will give my best to my family and trust God to sustain all else.

5. I will reflect on the goodness of God. His faithfulness will be the focus of my thoughts and conversation.

17

Fight for
the Quiet

> "In repentance and rest is your salvation, in quietness and trust is your strength."
>
> **ISAIAH 30:15**

The house is quiet, my favorite hot beverage is warm in my grip, and the blanket wrapped around me is offering the perfect amount of coziness. For the first time in a while, I get to experience the power of silence. Soon, though, my mind begins to wander. I reach for my phone. Recognizing my unhealthy attachment to it, I purpose to embrace stillness. Quiet. Deep breaths. As I choose to be with Jesus, I feel Him meet me. My heart is expectant because I know I've made space to actually hear Him.

God continually reminded us in His Word about the importance of solitude. When we have prioritized quiet time in our schedule, we often notice a difference in how we operate in our relationships or respond to change.

The truth is, solitude isn't something that just happens to us. It doesn't just slip into the rhythm of our routine. It's a choice we must make in every season, despite the countless distractions that come our way. God suggested solitude for a multitude of reasons, but first and foremost, He knows our souls desperately need it. He sees our exhaustion and hears our pleas for rest. Life feels like a balancing act, and we just want to experience some stability beneath our feet. The good news is, He offers that.

When you create space for quiet, you can draw near to Him. You learn to let go of the past, rest in the present, and trust God with what you need for the future. This week, let your mind dwell on the ways God has blessed you. In the past, how frequently did you pray for the exact situation you find yourself in now? The same God who has blessed you before is sure to bless you again. So as your circumstances stir stress, frustration, and impatience in your soul, return to the Lord in solitude. Silence your phone and lean into the greatest Communicator of all time—what does He have to say about your circumstances? What does your spirit need from the Great Supplier? You will never outrun His patience, outkick His provision, or outlast His ability to restore even the most broken situations. In solitude, you will not be reminded of your strength; you will be reminded of His.

Your God is sure about you. Maybe it's been some time since you've quieted your heart and let yourself be still with the Father. Don't let the Enemy steal another moment trying to convince you that shame or guilt is what the Father wants for your life. Come back to God. He longs to spend time with you. This week, He wants you to sit under the shadow of His wings so He can restore your strength, remind you of your assignment, and revive your passion and purpose.

Create space for solitude and watch as God meets you right where you are.

DECLARE OVER YOUR WEEK:

1. I will make room for quiet and allow my soul to breathe.

2. I will put down my phone and recognize the blessings right in front of me.

3. I will draw near to God. Abiding in Him, I find comfort, joy, and restorative strength.

4. My mood will not fluctuate with my circumstances; rather, my spirit will remain consistent and sure.

5. I will be generous with my knowledge, gifts, and resources, knowing that God has an endless supply.

18

God's Plan
› Mine

To acquire wisdom is to love yourself; people
who cherish understanding will prosper.

PROVERBS 19:8 NLT

I t was a beautiful day, and the playground was packed.
My son, Sledge, and I strolled and enjoyed watching
other families play made-up games and get their energy
out. My eyes landed on one little boy at the top of the
climbing structure. Glancing at his mama, I could see her
frightened face as she tried to redirect him. Sure enough,
his stubbornness to do as he pleased meant that he took a
tumble. I then watched the mother cleaning up her son's
scrapes and drying his tears. I wish it weren't the case, but
as I watched this child, I saw *myself.*

The truth is, it's hard to have a teachable spirit. It
requires a foundation of humility, a willingness to be
wrong, and a constant belief that godly wisdom is far supe-
rior to the desires, prayers, and temporary longings of your
human heart.

This week, there will be countless moments when
you'll face this decision: Will you hold tightly to your
pride and how you're perceived, or will you walk in humility, choosing to receive God's highest and best for your
life as you accept His correction? Whether the teachable
moments take place between you and your boss, you and

your spouse, or just between you and Jesus, being a student is one of the most powerful roles you get to claim as a child of God. Perfection is not the goal; progress is. Popularity isn't the goal; legacy is. Impressing the world isn't the goal; living impacted by Jesus and His truth is.

These truths, if you really believe them, can change everything about your week.

The rich and abundant life you have been promised and the one your heart deeply desires will always be found on the other side of refinement, no matter how painful or intense it may feel. Sometimes you'll want to throw in the towel. In those moments—or seasons—ask the Holy Spirit for endurance, patience, and a deeper hunger to live like Jesus. He will help you dig in and dig deep.

The choice to have a teachable spirit means operating in the belief that God is God, and you are not. He is the Teacher and you are the student. Receive His correction as a love letter to your soul, calling you back into the shadow of His wings and reminding you that His definition of "more" is the life you want to live.

DECLARE OVER YOUR WEEK:

1. I will receive constructive criticism with a humble and teachable spirit.

2. I will declare that my hands are open and my heart is willing to go wherever He leads.

3. I will remember that God is the game changer in my life.

4. I will trust that God's will is for my good, even when I don't understand what He is doing.

5. I will look forward to the life God has for me. Every day is a blessing.

19

Surrender the Shame

I can't go, but I so wish I could! I'm sorry, I'm just not feeling well." I was trying to convince my boyfriend that I couldn't attend the special weekend event with him. The truth? I was letting my shame bully me, because I hated how my skin looked. Knowing how petty I was being made me want to sink farther into the hole I had already made my home. *How can something so superficial be controlling decisions about my life?* As I made the decision, I hated the way I felt inside.

Can you recall a specific moment when you let fear or shame take the wheel?

It's interesting how we can know that something isn't helpful, true, or effective yet fall prey to it so easily. When Jesus told us that His mercy is new and that our sins are remembered no longer, He meant that very literally. We talk about freedom, but I wonder how many of us are tapping into the freedom that the Holy Spirit has offered to us.

This week, you get to make a choice every single day:

Will you release the shame or fear entangling you and embrace the freedom that God has for you?

Every person has their thorn, an area of their lives that tends to plague them or be the loudest when shame taps on the door. It could be in their work, their marriage, a previous addiction, their body image, or their financial situation. Jesus wants you to be aware of your thorn—not so He can shame you, but so that He can help you walk in healing, restoration, and hope.

Be willing to get honest about your thorn so that the Healer can work. Bring light to the dark places so that the great Restorer can do what only He can do. When you invite the Holy Spirit and trusted members of your inner circle into that place, you can better understand, treat, and implement practices that speak to the particulars.

No more being consumed about what others think of you (or what they *might* think of you). Immerse yourself in what your Maker says about you, what He believes about your future, and what He has equipped you with to fight the good fight this week.

Release shame from your shoulders. Turn to the Holy Spirit in everything you say and do. Treat yourself and others with compassion, and walk in the present moment. Do those things, and you will experience the freedom you've been longing to taste.

DECLARE OVER YOUR WEEK:

1. Refusing to be bullied by shame, I will welcome the Holy Spirit into every conversation and every space.

2. I will let Jesus bear my burdens.

3. I will treat my body with compassion, kindness, and gentleness.

4. I will release any guilt or shame from my past so that I can be fully present.

5. I will stop trying to manage others' perceptions of me, and I will immerse myself in my Maker's proclamations over me.

20

Unshakable
Sovereignty

And Jesus came and said to them, "All authority
in heaven and on earth has been given to me."
MATTHEW 28:18 ESV

When the judge walks in, everyone stops and notices. Her footsteps are heard throughout the courtroom, and her eyes are locked on those whose futures she will soon determine. With her gavel in hand, her presence communicates *authority*.

When you think of the word *authority*, what comes to mind? Do you tend to link it with exercising courage and experiencing victory, or do you often associate it with discipline and punishment?

Instead of trusting our heavenly Father's authority over our day, sometimes it's easier to complain and focus on the circumstances of our daily life. Maybe the goals we're seeking are genuinely good—we'd like some extra income to pay for childcare, we'd like a new car to make sure we have a reliable way to commute to work every day, or we're looking for an opportunity to move closer to family. These are all good things to work toward, but sometimes our desires become our obsessions. In times like these, we must remind ourselves of the One who has authority over where we've been, where we currently stand, and the place where we're going.

This week, be intentional about accepting God's guidance in every thought, word, and action. Before you sit down with your family to eat dinner, decide that you will offer life-giving conversation, words that build up and edify rather than tear down and destroy. As you clean up around the house, prepare for meetings at work, or carry on with your mundane tasks, choose to operate in excellence. It is often the obedience in the monotonous parts of life that ushers in the sweetest moments between you and the Holy Spirit, as you learn to trust His strength in you more and more.

Life will have its trials—that is promised. However, when you remember who has authority over your story, the trials become catalysts for newfound strength and opportunities to experience God's faithfulness. When unexpected moments occur this week, turn to the unchanging Word of God and plant yourself in His promises. You get to rest in the truth that you belong to God and that there is no circumstance, no person, no struggle, and no stronghold that could prevent that from being true. How reassuring is that?

God is with you, and His authority over your life is absolute. On Christ the solid Rock, you stand.

DECLARE OVER YOUR WEEK:

1. I will rest in the fact that I belong to God, and He has all authority.

2. I will thank God for the breath in my lungs and the future He's planned for me.

3. No matter what, I will operate with excellence and grace because I am working for God, not for people.

4. I will apply the filter of truth over every thought I have.

5. I will keep my heart encouraged with the infallible, life-changing Word of God.

Equipped for Hard Things

Count it all joy . . . when you meet trials of
various kinds, for you know that the testing
of your faith produces steadfastness. And let
steadfastness have its full effect, that you may
be perfect and complete, lacking in nothing.

JAMES 1:2–4 ESV

Cleere, you have a choice here. You can either be Sledge's mom, or you can try to be his nurse." I could feel the shift, as if Jesus were sitting there in the hospital room with me. We had been in the hospital for only three weeks, and baby Sledge did not yet even weigh three pounds. I knew the journey was far from over. My son would be cared for by hundreds of medical professionals during his stay, but there was only one person graced and equipped to be his mama. It felt like the hardest thing ever to surrender and trust the process, but I knew it was the only way I could steward this season well.

The truth is, we are capable of doing hard things. Seasons of uncertainty were never meant to be the exception to a comfortable, easy, predictable life; they are what life is, forcing us to realize our need. Our pride usually requires hard things to learn the art of trusting and depending on God, realizing we can't do anything good on our own. Our discomfort welcomes the presence of the

Comforter and becomes a gateway to experiencing His deep mercy.

This week, you get to be available to the Most High, our wonderful and loving heavenly Father. The beautiful thing about submitting your timeline, desires, and deepest prayers to Him is that He already knows all those things. He is aware of what you want but even more aware of what you truly need. As you make yourself fully available to do His will, He will align your desires with His, molding you into His image and transforming you into the person He created you to be.

It's okay if you don't want to do the hard thing— the Holy Spirit will always help you do the holy thing. Whether it's finishing a task you feel ill-prepared to do, showing up for an appointment where you fear the news you'll receive, or standing firm in a situation or relationship where it would be easier to cave, you have His undivided attention and care this week.

You have been prepared for this place, you are protected in this place, and God will provide for you in this place. As you wake up, as you work, and as you walk forward into the unknown, take heart in knowing that you have been equipped to do the hard things.

DECLARE OVER YOUR WEEK:

1. I will remember that I am capable of doing hard things because nothing is too hard for God.

2. I will wake up with gratitude, work with grit, and walk with grace.

3. I will offer God my constant availability, trusting Him with my time, resources, and dreams.

4. I will discipline my emotions and let the Word of God give me a sound mind.

5. I will praise God for how He has equipped me for this place—right here, right now.

Joy While
You Wait

When I was starting to write and create products, I remember feeling silly and vulnerable, and I found myself asking, "Am I crazy for thinking this will work?" Then, after years of digging, plowing, and showing up when the harvest felt distant, the sales began to increase, and people began to share my content. My motivation really was to share the kindness of God and expand His family; however, it's only human nature to wonder if we're driving in the right direction when there aren't many signs on the journey! Now I see the wait was the preparation. No matter the outcome, I learned that God is trustworthy. Do you find it hard to remain joyful when you're waiting for something you really, really want? When God's timeline seems delayed, do you feel discouraged about moving forward?

As believers, we understand that true joy is not dependent on circumstances or answered prayers. Joy comes when we know the heart of the Controller of all circumstances and the Hearer of all prayers. This means that no matter the situation, joy is possible. Cultivating joy isn't automatic or easy; it is a discipline rooted in the belief that God is good, He is for us, and His timeline can be trusted.

This week, you will come up against your own internal clock and wonder, *Where is God? Does He see me?* In each of those moments, you will have the opportunity to walk in faith and cultivate a joy that isn't dependent on His answering your prayers or delivering your desires. Rather, this joy is possible because you believe that He is who He says He is. Make Him the cornerstone of your life, and you will be comforted by His faithfulness no matter how intensely the waves crash around you.

When your belief feels shaky, go back to His Word. Dig deep into what He has already promised you. Chances are, the very thing you are waiting for will not be the transformation you are hoping for. But how you wait right now will become the highway to the holiness your soul has been craving. God is a loving God, and He would never withhold a good thing from you.

As you surrender your own preference and realign with your heavenly Father's perspective, patience refuels your soul. Be encouraged and remember: His timeline is the one you would always pick if you knew what He knows and could see what He sees.

Don't forget: this life is simply a short moment on your way to forever. Don't be frustrated with the wait; commit to choosing joy.

DECLARE OVER YOUR WEEK:

1. If I have to wait, I will do so with patience and trust, knowing that God never withholds His best from me.

2. I will remember that God's timeline is perfect.

3. Because God's faithfulness is the root of my celebration, I will choose joy every day.

4. I will keep my heart encouraged with the living Word of God—it is relevant to every situation.

5. Remarkable kindness, lavish grace, and radical faith will be my goals this week.

23

The Power of Your Perspective

I f I could have one superpower, it would be to be able to see like the Father sees. Because if I could see myself and others and the world around me through the lens of my Father, my insecurity would cease, my compassion would increase, peace would flood my soul, and wisdom would guide me. If I were given such an amazing gift, I *hope* I would do everything in my power to bring heaven to earth and help others see with fresh eyes.

The lens through which we view our lives has everything to do with how we choose to respond, what decisions we make, and how we love others. Think about this: it's possible for two people to exist in the same room, experiencing the same scenario, and have two very different perspectives. So who's right? The answer is determined by whether the filter we hold is one that prioritizes heaven or treasures the things of this world.

This week, you'll have the privilege of building a perspective on the unchanging Word of God and the infallible hope of heaven. This means that when distractions tempt, culture condemns, Instagram incites, or fear tries to make you forget who is in control, you get to refocus your eyes on the One who stills the seas. Be aware of the triggers that tend to taint your perspective and guard your heart against them. It's not harsh to create boundaries that help you protect your peace and prioritize Jesus; that's the most caring thing you can do for yourself.

As situations arise, conversations are had, and crossroads come into play, take the time to get away and look at your life from heaven's view. You are never too busy to pause, assess, realign, and reprioritize. From heaven's view, you'll find greater endurance as you remember that your struggle is temporary. You'll receive an infusion of strength, an innovative mind to create, and an invitation to rest in the arms that will never let you go. His eyes are always on your life.

Elevate your perspective, and it will change your whole life.

DECLARE OVER YOUR WEEK:

1. Recognizing that my perspective is my passport, I will let it elevate my faith instead of escalating my fear.

2. I will guard my heart from anything that doesn't help me become more like Jesus.

3. With gratitude on my lips, I will not let the trap of unrealistic expectations ruin my experience.

4. I will fill myself with things that help my words be kind, my actions be obedient, and my posture remain humble.

5. Declaring growth in areas where I've been stagnant, I will break through the places where I've been struggling and discover strength where I've felt weak.

24

Recalibrating with the Holy Spirit

> For the moment all discipline seems painful rather than pleasant, but later it yields the peaceful fruit of righteousness to those who have been trained by it.
> **HEBREWS 12:11** ESV

She *loved* her job. That is, she loved it until a new coworker came along. Suddenly, my friend, who is easily the most peaceable, tenderhearted, and gracious human, was trying to navigate how to operate in tight quarters with someone who regularly hurt her feelings and didn't offer much understanding as to why. She was fighting for peace but asking, "What do you do when you feel like the other person prefers stress and tension?" That's a hard question, isn't it?

Do we take a moment to pause before responding to a challenging person or situation? Wisdom tells us to give it a moment—to take our foot off the gas pedal and recalibrate our perspective from a heavenly lens.

The Holy Spirit helps us to recalibrate! As He whispers to our soul and speaks truth over our heart, we'll find direction for the next step forward. The greatest lie the Enemy will tell us is that we have to earn the power of the Holy Spirit—but He has already been given to us as a gift from the Father. There is no level of elite faith, no impeccable performance, or no accolade we could offer that would earn the grace that is given through Him. He is love personified. He is strength when we are weak, perseverance when we want to run, hope when we feel lost, and peace when our life feels in disarray.

This week, will you model Jesus in your heart and your home and your workplace, or will you be molded by culture and the world around you? Remember, you have been given a spirit of self-control in your thoughts, words, and actions; claim this and walk in it. When your worries begin to snowball or when your body goes into fight-or-flight, turn to Scripture. Speak its truth out loud and watch Jesus permeate your space. When you make room for Him, He brings life and assurance to every place.

A compassionate heart and a warm spirit aren't personality traits you're simply born with. You gain these attributes when you yield to the Holy Spirit in everything you do. Having a heart of wisdom does not mean you know everything; it means that you surrender moment by moment to the One who does.

Yield. The Spirit is near, and He will help you.

DECLARE OVER YOUR WEEK:

1. I will yield to the Holy Spirit in everything I do.

2. I will be intentional about preparing my heart for the week, keeping what matters at the top of my to-do list.

3. Speaking Scripture over my soul, I will recognize when I am tempted to react unlovingly.

4. I will model Jesus in my home first and foremost, operating with a warm spirit, a compassionate heart, and a constant focus on the One who keeps it all together.

5. I will practice self-control with my words, replacing criticism with praise over myself and others.

25

A Harvest Worth Waiting For

> And let us not grow weary of doing good, for in
> due season we will reap, if we do not give up.
>
> **GALATIANS 6:9** ESV

B attling infertility, struggling to understand the why behind the wait and the purpose behind the pain, my dear friend was on her fourth round of in vitro fertilization. Despite the difficult reality of her situation, she was doing everything she could to walk in hope. As I prayed and sought words to encourage her spirit, I found myself also asking, "Jesus, why hasn't it happened yet? How do I encourage her in a way that is helpful?"

Sometimes, the seasons that we thought would be brief feel like they've become the norm and we need a sign that God is still bringing life to the fields that are our lives.

The truth is, no one wants us to experience a fruitful life more than the One who establishes the work of our hands. From a practical standpoint, it will help us to think this through: Would it benefit God to withhold goodness from those He loves? If His goal is our growth and transformation, why would He be stingy about what He provides, especially when His supply is unlimited?

The heart of the question then becomes, Do we believe God is trustworthy? Do we believe He is for us? If we're unsure about His faithfulness, the timeline of our harvest and the purpose of our work will always feel shaky, threatened, and unfair. Sometimes the answer to our restlessness for more is walking in gratitude for the grace He has already extended to us. A heart that is ripe for harvest is one that recognizes it never deserved the ground it was given in the first place.

This week, choose to believe that the ultimate Farmer is on your case. Take a walk outside and breathe the air deep into your lungs. Do you feel that? His mercy is full, and His faithfulness is new every morning. The same God who provides for the lilies of the field is the One who is watching over you—His favorite creation.

Let go of expectations from others so you can meet your deepest needs. Refresh your memory with the knowledge that all seasons are both necessary and temporary. When the rain comes, it will help you grow; it will not last forever. When the scorching heat feels oppressive, think ahead to the cool air you know is coming.

The greatest harvest is not what God is doing with your hands or what you can see in front of you. The most life-changing harvest is what God is doing with your heart.

DECLARE OVER YOUR WEEK:

1. I will trust God with the timing of the harvest. Waiting on God is always worth it.

2. I will begin my day with worship, letting the sovereignty of Jesus calm my heart.

3. I will depend on God, not humans, to meet my deepest needs.

4. I will take a walk and let the beauty of the world around me remind my soul that hope is on the horizon.

5. I will believe God is at work in my home and in the world around me.

26

Declutter Your Thought Life

> Finally, brothers and sisters, whatever is true, whatever is noble, whatever is right, whatever is pure, whatever is lovely, whatever is admirable—if anything is excellent or praiseworthy—think about such things.
>
> **PHILIPPIANS 4:8**

I magine a room filled with a million sticky notes. They all contain reminders, to-dos, goals, and what-ifs to consider. Feels cluttered and chaotic, doesn't it? That's how my mind felt as I started on a walk to get outside the introspective bubble I'd been hanging out in for far too long. On my walk I caught myself forming snowballs of assumptions about a relationship in my life. Suddenly, I knew it was time to do something different. Some clearing, renewing, and refreshing needed to happen, and it wasn't going to happen in the confines of my own mind.

The Enemy often uses a trick when it comes to our minds. He likes to convince us that if a thought knocks on our door, we invited it and should let it in. We need to give it a seat at our table and entertain it with conversation. However, Scripture tells us we'll have many thoughts that must be captured, not hosted by our hearts.

Whether consciously or subconsciously, your mind is continually being molded by the things you see, experience, read, listen to, entertain, and process. Your brain is truly a sponge—brilliant and effective in nature, but only when it's protected, cleaned out, and used for purposes that fit its design and creation. It was not meant to travel a million miles a minute, receive constant overstimulation, and focus on a thousand things at once.

The first step to protect your thought life is to understand what the Maker desired for it to be. He yearns for you to experience the purity, strength, and wholeness that come from a well-guarded mind. He desires you to meditate on His truth, anchor yourself in self-control, and abide in His promises for your life.

Productivity and peace will follow when you attend to the basic calling on your life—loving God and loving others. Everything else can wait. And sure, God knows you can't ignore reality. But you always have time to stop and ask the Holy Spirit to quiet your racing thoughts and provide guidance with the next step forward.

Do what you must to protect your thought life. Cancel some appointments or make some new ones. Soak in the sunshine. Journal. Let your number one priority determine every other particular in your life, and you'll find newfound energy and a focused mind to show up where He calls you.

You become a summary of your thoughts—make them good, praiseworthy, and true.

DECLARE OVER YOUR WEEK:

1. I will channel my thoughts toward what is true, kind, and praiseworthy.

2. Every morning I will ask, *What will matter in eternity?* I will prioritize that.

3. I will quiet my mind and limit my social media use, knowing my input always affects my output.

4. I will create margin to soak in the sunshine and do things that bring me joy and peace.

5. I will savor the present instead of obsessing over the future.

Follow the Shepherd; Leave the Herd

W e have probably all experienced that moment when we recognize someone isn't a huge fan of us, and we aren't sure how to respond or what caused that opinion to form. While we want to change their opinion, we're acutely aware we have no control over it. I remember sorting through this thought process when I was starting my business, Cleerely Stated, and feeling a little misunderstood by someone I knew; I was either going to let her incorrect assumptions hold me hostage, or I was going to run forth and let God's voice be louder. Despite the strangling feeling of being judged, I was reminded that our hearts only discover freedom when we actually let others' judgment go.

Isn't it interesting how much of the world around us is built on the opinion of others? From the fashion choices we make to the books we read to the definition of *success* we hold, who is determining how we live?

The herd mentality is an interesting phenomenon. The more our brain perceives something is liked by the masses, the more we assume it's worthy of our time and resources. But the truth is, we were never created to follow the herd. We were made to follow the Shepherd. The restlessness inside our souls is not because we're unable to meet the world's standards; it's because we were made for a different standard.

Only one Voice can speak to our soul and remind us of our security. Being a child of the King means that He loves us even before we do a single thing. His claim over us isn't because of our choices but because of His character. When we begin to operate as a beloved child of Jesus, we can then serve others not *for* their love but *out of* love. This is a game changer.

Do you feel like you have an accurate idea of the way Jesus sees you? Which aspects of your life feel driven by the desire to fit in? These questions aren't meant to shame you. They're designed to protect your soul. When judgments from others make you feel tired, lonely, or stressed, go back to the ultimate Source. Let your Maker—the One who determines your identity—speak life over you.

This week, you get to walk in the truth of this statement: Jesus is already proud of you. As you sit with the Holy Spirit and ask for greater revelations of God's love for you, you will learn to trust His opinion more and more. The more you believe God's opinion about you, the less you will feel offended by the world's opinions, criticism, and lack of understanding. This makes you wildly effective for building His kingdom.

Your identity is not in jeopardy, nor does it need to be earned—just embraced.

DECLARE OVER YOUR WEEK:

1. I will remember that I am loved by God today, even before I do a single thing.

2. I will seek to serve others, not impress them.

3. When I feel lonely, tired, or stressed, I will go to Jesus—the only Refreshment I need.

4. I will stand in agreement with what Jesus says about my past, present, and future.

5. I will ask God to reveal the specific ways He loves me, and I will take time to receive them.

Guardrails That Bring Peace

He led me to a place of safety; he rescued
me because he delights in me.

PSALM 18:19 NLT

I magine the "yard" that is your life. It has all that you need, everything good and beneficial, and it provides protection from anything that might harm you. The boundary set by the Father is the fence around your yard. And although there is chaos and noise beyond those guardrails, you know that the only place life is found is where He has instructed you to play, go, be, and live.

When you think about the word *boundaries*, what adjectives come to mind? Do they feel harsh or helpful?

It's important to think about our positive or negative connotations around this concept because they determine our actions. For example, if we believe boundaries are harsh and add rigidity to our life, we will not want to implement them. On the flip side, if we view boundaries as helpful and efficient for living the abundant life we know we were called to live, we will welcome them, regardless of the challenges they may present.

Where we set our boundaries reveals what's most important to us. Maybe we want to set a boundary to protect our time at home with our family, or perhaps we want to set firm guidelines around how we spend our money.

But setting these boundaries might mean we'll disappoint our employer, friends, or someone we admire—and so we resist. We don't follow through on our boundaries because the consequences feel too great; we prioritize short-term comfort over long-term gain.

For the one who struggles to set boundaries, there is good news. Your heavenly Father draws boundary lines only for your good and His glory. When you trust Jesus' boundary lines set forth in His Word and implement that instruction, you will experience the freedom, contentment, and peace that inhabit that territory. These lines prevent burnout, provide for your gifts, and protect your purpose.

Freedom is not found through the absence of boundaries; it's discovered through them. In a broken world, boundaries take intention. So don't drift into the land of good intentions. Decide to implement rhythms that help you live a life you're passionate about. Rather than reacting to the world around you, slow your pace and set boundaries that protect your mind against comparison, burnout, and stress. What good is it if you gain the whole world and lose your soul?

So let this week be different. Enjoy the beauty and safety of exactly where you are as you draw the boundaries God has for you. This will change your life.

DECLARE OVER YOUR WEEK:

1. I will set boundaries that protect my peace and direct my energy toward what truly matters.

2. Before my feet hit the floor, I will declare life over my present and confidence over my future.

3. I will have hard conversations, knowing that Jesus will show me when to speak and when to be quiet.

4. I will remember that my words bring death or life. I choose life.

5. I will slow down my pace, set realistic expectations, and remember the importance of enjoying my current season.

29

Doing the
Deep Work

Physical training is good, but training for
godliness is much better, promising benefits
in this life and in the life to come.

1 TIMOTHY 4:8 NLT

It's interesting to consider how Jesus would live in the current times. How would He handle social media, the pressure to look a certain way, or the immense focus on outward appearance?

It's common for people to spend hours curating their Instagram posts, applying filters that don't resemble reality, and exhausting themselves with creating pictures of their lives they can't sustain. The truth is, there is a stirring in our souls to live a life filled with lovely, lasting things. This stirring can disguise itself as restlessness or fear of missing out. We may feel a tension between living in this world and not being made for it, but that tension is really a gift. It's a knock on the window of our souls that whispers, *You were made for more.*

This week, there is something much better than projecting an impressive picture of your life to the watching world. Instead, you have the opportunity to walk in the transformative power of the Holy Spirit.

When you feel like you don't measure up to the expectations of the world, recognize that this is a chance to lean into the faithfulness of God. When your heart feels frustrated or frazzled, cling to the peace of God and let it transcend whatever you're feeling or facing; He is your calm in the storm. When you focus on the work Jesus is doing inside you, hardship feels less like an enemy and more like a teacher, transforming you from the inside out.

Sometimes the hard and holy work of transformation looks like changing what you say yes to. Sometimes it means getting serious about therapy with your spouse or no longer avoiding your health issues. The deep roots of these tensions are challenging and often uncomfortable, but they are the greatest work of your life. Thank God for how He is opening your eyes, refining your heart, and helping you build a life outside your own bubble.

There is nothing richer than a life committed to the process of sanctification, knowing that the eternal reward you will gain is worth any pain you'll experience on this earth. It's interesting how life changes when you switch your focus from this moment to your legacy. Lasting fruit is the promise of a heart rooted in Jesus.

So this week, breathe. Consider the cross before every word you say and every action you take, letting the truth of forever change everything about how you operate now. That kind of life far outlives you.

DECLARE OVER YOUR WEEK:

1. I will focus my attention on my inward work of transformation rather than my outward appearance.

2. Jesus will be the center of my life in all areas.

3. I will release the pressure to curate a pristine perception of my life and focus on building a legacy instead.

4. I will recognize that disappointment, frustration, and hardship are all opportunities to grow in strength, trust, and patience.

5. I will take moments to breathe, recognize God's hand, and thank Him for every way He is aligning my heart with His.

30

The Power of Unseen Places

For if someone does not know how to manage his
own household, how will he care for God's church?
1 TIMOTHY 3:5 ESV

W e put together the outfit that is sure to impress,
get dressed, and arrive at our destination. We
join conversations, but we're really busy trying
to capture the perfect selfie of the experience. The tiny
square we filter and post looks beautiful, but we feel more
than a little empty. The more frequently we do this, the
more we crave being known for the life we're really living
instead of being admired for the life we're curating.

How much time do you spend curating a life rather
than living one? Do you find it easier to focus on the
aspects of your life that are seen by others and push the
hidden ones to the side?

Due to our overstimulating world (thanks, social
media), we tend to prioritize what's on the surface more
than what's growing underneath. And when we do that,
we often carry burdens we were never supposed to carry,
preventing us from living the life we *were* created to live.
Whether it's the pressure to be liked by everyone or to
measure up to perfection, the world will consume our
energy with unimportant things. This week, we get to walk
with the wisdom that the unseen can be a powerful and

purposeful place for our energy to reside. It is our diligence to the mundane tasks, our attention to the little things, and our commitment to the present that God honors.

If you are feeling unseen and unappreciated, don't let the Enemy convince you that it translates to your being unimportant. When you remain steadfast in the seemingly mundane things, God is honored, and your character is built. Decide now that your focus will be on what matters in eternity, knowing it affects everything about the visible. Commit to showing up and staying the course, even when it's more popular to leave.

This week, prioritize your mental health and be willing to let go of anything that doesn't align with your God-given assignment to follow Him and make disciples. Allow space for your soul to breathe so you can remember that pleasing Him is always your top priority. Ask Him to help you let go of the "glamorous" life and replace it with a deep hunger for a surrendered one.

Even when you feel unseen, you're not invisible—because there's Someone who sees you in your most vulnerable moments, and He loves you so much. Choose to let His eyes be enough.

As you work toward what He prioritizes this week—the unseen moments of service, the unappreciated grace you offer to others, the quiet moments of learning about His heart that reverberate across your life—continue to show up and do the deep work of the soul. Because you know the abundant life is worth whatever it asks of you.

DECLARE OVER YOUR WEEK:

1. I will yearn to lead a surrendered life that is rooted in confidence in the living God.

2. I will let God's grace blanket my life.

3. I will prioritize my mental health, even when it's hard or uncomfortable.

4. I will be a person of integrity, even when no one is looking or noticing.

5. I will seek to be a faithful student before I expect to be a fearless leader.

31

The Posture
of Victory

For the LORD your God is the one who
goes with you to fight for you against
your enemies to give you victory.

DEUTERONOMY 20:4

Here's something I've noticed about myself: my expectations affect my perspective. How I expect something to go determines my excitement about it, my countenance when discussing it, and often my strength when enduring it. Have you noticed this same theme in your own life?

With every trial we face, our perspective is shaped by whether we believe God is fighting on our behalf. When we believe we have the advantage, we see obstacles as opportunities and our gifts as tools, and we live with a peace that reaches far beyond what we can see. On the flip side, when we believe we are operating at a disadvantage, any setback feels like a setup for failure. People become interruptions, and we find ourselves struggling to understand our purpose.

How do you know which battle stance you're operating from? Survey your everyday moments and how you approach difficult circumstances. Do you constantly fear what's around the bend, worried that bad news or a bigger Goliath awaits you? Do you recognize your gifts and the

125

gifts of others as a team effort to expand the kingdom of heaven? The victorious mindset is one that continually sets eternity at the forefront.

This week, you get to choose your posture. That will shape your perspective and ultimately determine your peace.

When frustration arises or something threatens your ability to keep moving forward, go to the throne. God's battle plan includes every pivot that leads to walking in the greatest promise you will ever know. Hold your head up and run with endurance, anticipation, and great hope. He is working behind the scenes in ways you cannot see. Remind your soul that He will provide discernment and clarity when your emotions try to lead the charge. Move in confidence that's based on His character, not your circumstance—He has never lost a battle.

So stand on this truth and ask for wisdom on how to show up each day, what to bring, and when to move. God is already there for the medical diagnosis up ahead, the work situation you didn't foresee, the relationship struggle you didn't predict, or whatever else you may face. Your victory has been established, sealed, and solidified by the Name above all names. Whom or what shall you fear?

Give yourself permission to approach difficult situations as if you're operating from a place of victory. Let the King determine your battle stance because He already gave you the banner over your life: *victory*. Receive it.

DECLARE OVER YOUR WEEK:

1. I will visualize God's victory ahead and run with endurance, hope, and strength.

2. I will fuel my body, renew my mind, and encourage my heart with life-giving things.

3. I will bring my frustrations to the Lord's throne instead of the phone and ask Him for help.

4. I will trust God's protection and provision over my emotions, health, family, and future. He is sure and absolute.

5. I will look for God's hand in every space. He is moving, and I trust everything He does.

32

A Spirit of
Excellence

D id that meet their expectations? Could I have done more? *Should* I have done more?" I was talking to myself as I prepared for bed and finally laid my head down on the pillow after a long, exhausting day. Things hadn't gone perfectly, but I knew I had done everything possible with the capacity I had and the resources given to me. In that moment I felt Jesus meet me, quiet my mind, and assure me, *That's all I ask of you. Leave the rest up to Me.*

We were made in the image of God, and our hearts were made to pursue the character of Jesus. We will always need to combat the desire to control what isn't ours, and we will often be consumed by our own worries rather than serving those around us. The good news? God is fully aware of this daily tension, and because of that, He has gifted us with the Holy Spirit. He has prepared us in advance to fight the good fight of faith, walking with the Spirit and living in a way that intentionally points to Jesus whether life feels hopeful or hard.

Work will not always be fun or exciting. That's okay. Because we are working for God, we get to show up with excellence and anticipation, fully trusting that the Miracle Worker is always moving amid the mundane. Our minds will want to venture into areas of our lives that feel uncertain and try to exert control; in these moments, we must remind our souls of the Good Shepherd, the One who is shifting, sorting out, and stewarding everything for our good.

This week, begin your days by communicating with Jesus—in song, in prayer, and in gratitude. Let your heart be reminded of His steadfast character and ask Him for His help to show up with the same steadfastness in every situation, knowing that He will always see your integrity and consistency. Instead of dreading the obligations before you, remember the importance of hard work and recalibrate your mind to appreciate the sweat that brings sanctification. Open your eyes to those around you as you get outside your own head. Make sure they know how much you care.

The favor, strength, and abundant joy your soul craves is satisfied in your relationship with Jesus. With this in mind, do your best work, whatever that may be, and rest easy.

Intentionality and excellence—may they be the desires for your heart and hands as you bring heaven to earth.

DECLARE OVER YOUR WEEK:

1. Being intentional, seeking excellence, I will begin my days by talking to Jesus.

2. I will remember that I am not what I do, but I will joyfully work hard in all that I do.

3. I will take responsibility for what is in my control and surrender what is not.

4. I will check in on those around me and make sure they know how much I care.

5. I will embrace all that God has called me to be. Favor, strength, and joy are mine.

33

Staying in
Your Lane

M rs. Cleere, I can't do flips like them and I lost my glitter scrunchie." I watched as her little head sank lower and she turned to walk back to me in the waiting area. My precious Molly girl, whom I had the joy of babysitting when I was in college, was struggling with comparing herself to other gymnasts. In that moment, I could see myself in sweet Molly. I understood her struggle. Why is it that we so quickly criticize ourselves for what we lack, who we aren't, or what we can't do instead of recognizing the treasure we are, the gifts we do have, and the truth of our identity as His children?

When we look at others, our preconceived notions are based on what those people have curated for us to see— controlled and crafted to impress. From gymnastics to careers to relationships and everything in between, things are not always as they appear. From the outside looking in, we may not be aware of the work it took that person to get where they are: the late nights, the emotions swirling beneath the surface, the hiccups that accompanied their journey, and the deep work they've done. This is one reason why God wants us to serve others, not judge them: our service and curiosity are invitations to learning more about who they really are. Chances are, when we invest in hearing someone's story, our previous assumptions will go out the window.

This week, you may find yourself distracted from what you know God has called you to do. As you sit with Jesus and let Him order your day, ask Him to show you the next right thing to do. You'll have hurdles to jump, obstacles to overcome, and clutter to clear from your path; that has already been promised by God. Heed this wisdom so you can effectively respond with the gifts, strength, and passion inside you. When the ground is no longer flat, push yourself to keep going. As God's supernatural strength settles into your space, He will lift you up and carry you forward.

Season your words with kindness, over yourself and over the lives of others. Look for opportunities to love people right where they are without comparing your life to theirs. The remedy to comparison is not avoiding others or refusing to learn about their lives. The cure is being so secure in God's heart for you that you trust His timing, His ways, and His plans, whatever the assignments include.

Focus ahead, with your faith intact and your feet planted in your lane. The best is yet to come.

DECLARE OVER YOUR WEEK:

1. Rather than comparing myself to others, I will discern, accept, and trust what God is calling me to.

2. I will not try to fix those around me. I will focus on loving them just as they are.

3. I will remember that God fights for me and let that give me courage to keep going.

4. I will season my words with kindness, tenderness, and truth. Gossip will not be a part of my life.

5. I will place all my faith in the character of God. It has never failed me.

34

Love Without Expectation

"By this everyone will know that you are
my disciples, if you love one another."
JOHN 13:35

I watched my friend as she interacted with everyone who came through her front door, offering kindness and a warm hug to each one. Although she'd been suffering from a chronic illness, she radiated joy. It was my friend's birthday, and it didn't surprise me at all that there wasn't enough space to house all those who came to celebrate. This friend cheers others on, she is the first to pray for others when they need it, and she speaks life over people in a way that lets them know she has already discussed it with the Father.

Jesus also lived a life that was all about other people. Whether it was feeding the five thousand, speaking to the woman at the well, or walking on water with Peter, His heart was always focused on serving, sanctifying, and shepherding His flock. The interesting thing is that Jesus could have used His power to live a lavish life, dining with the most influential people and creating a comfortable existence for Himself separated from society. But He was not concerned with fulfilling the world's idea of "powerful" or "wealthy." His eyes were on His heavenly Father, knowing that His assignment was to help the very ones who were denying His existence.

You, exactly where you are right now, are in the perfect position to love those around you with kingdom kindness, persistent patience, and generous gentleness. There is nothing richer than a life built around extending God's family and expanding heaven.

This week, you'll constantly be met with the question "Will you love others like your Father does?" Jesus, until His final breath on the cross, put the needs of others before Himself. Through His example, you see that when you live like this, God always provides for you. Make serving your priority and spreading the gospel your mission, stripping away any ulterior motives so that you simply love others. When you ask, "How are you?" stick around to care about the answer. Be intentional with your conversation so you can seek to see others as Jesus does.

Remember, you have been saved by a love you could never earn or deserve. And the best way you could respond? Pay that love forward. Don't be so consumed by the destination ahead that you miss the people along the way—people are always the point when Jesus is the focus. Patience, gentleness, and kindness are always beneficial to the giver and the receiver.

Just love—even when it's complicated, when it's messy, when it's hard, and when it's uncomfortable. Why? Because you are all those things too.

DECLARE OVER YOUR WEEK:

1. I will remember that loving others is loving God.

2. I will not take the presence of others for granted.

3. When I ask others, "How are you?" I will listen and care about their answer.

4. I will choose patience over frustration, gentleness over harshness, and kindness over judgment.

5. I will go the extra mile to serve others, remembering that the point of my life is to love God and love others.

35

The Voice Worth Following

> Know that the LORD, He is God; it is He who
> has made us, and not we ourselves; we are
> His people and the sheep of His pasture.
> **PSALM 100:3 NKJV**

I promise it's about to level out. Trust me, it's worth the view. You're obsessed with sunsets—come on!" We were on a hike—a mild *two-hour* hike—and my hangry spirit was ready to be done. My brother and I kept going, and sure enough, the clearing appeared, and there it was: a cotton-candy sunset that you can't capture with a camera. Worth every bead of sweat! The simplest but truest reminder came as I took in the view: when you trust who you're following, you find perseverance for the journey.

Would you be willing to follow someone into the unknown if you didn't trust their heart? When you really trust someone, are you comfortable following them wherever they lead, even when the direction feels unclear?

Jesus is the Good Shepherd. When Scripture calls Him "the Shepherd," it is not referring to the kind of caretaker who lazily tends to the masses and hopes the danger will stay far away. Instead, He calls us each by name and pursues us one by one. When we pray, He hears us as if we are the only one talking to Him. He patiently hangs on our every word, delights in our nearness, and adoringly cares for our heart. We will never be a number to the One who calls us by name.

This week, unknowns will be at every corner. Even for the circumstances you feel like you've navigated before, life has a way of throwing curveballs and forcing detours. But you don't have to worry or fear what's around the bend. Remember that you have the Good Shepherd, the ultimate Guide, the constant Provider, and the Knower of all things with you and protecting you from all sides. When you cry out, you are not left wondering if He cares enough to respond. You can be fully confident that there is nothing more important to the Shepherd than His sheep.

When the field feels mundane, ordinary, and unimportant this week, keep showing up. Wherever God has you—in whatever place and position you hold—He has prepared the way. His plan is wise, and your purpose is significant. Let God determine where you go, who you listen to, what you believe, and how you live. The One who is leading you is The Way; He is incapable of leading you astray. You hear His voice, you know His gentleness, and you trust His heart—that is all you need.

Follow the Good Shepherd and let His unwavering devotion to your care be the source of your confidence.

DECLARE OVER YOUR WEEK:

1. Convinced that the Shepherd has never led me astray, I will trust Him today.

2. I will let my allegiance to God determine my alignment with everything else.

3. I will believe that I can hear the voice of God.

4. I will surrender my hurt, fear, and worry to the Good Shepherd.

5. I will approach the everyday rhythms of life with anticipation, passion, and faithfulness.

The Detours
That Save
You

Every day I checked for updates on my friend and her precious family as they navigated an unexpected medical diagnosis for one of her children. I was blown away by their faith. Many days there were more steps taken back than taken forward. Yet, her resolve was sure. When taking lunch to her one day, I asked, "How are you staying so steady?" I knew, but I also didn't. Her response? "I can either imagine my life without my child or with him still here. To me, there is only one choice." Faith, no matter how she felt, was the only way for her to survive. There was no other choice.

Isn't it funny how much we desire growth, yet how frequently we pray for comfort? Aren't seasons of change often when we grow the most in our faith?

We often choose to remain comfortable, coasting along with minimal waves, almost falling asleep on the lake of life. But Jesus knows a better and different way. His route incorporates more change than we'd prefer, knowing that change prompts us to reassess our foundation and remember our dependence on Him. Whether it be an unexpected relationship hurdle, a friendship that evolved differently than we thought, a job switch that caught us by surprise, or life's circumstances taking a sudden pivot, the constant in every situation is the One whose presence never changes.

It is one thing to remain faithful when we understand why something is happening, but true faith is the decision to trust God's faithfulness no matter how choppy the waters get. His protection over our lives is absolute, and through every shift in our journey, we learn to trust Him more. The detour is usually the part of the journey that offers the richest revelation and strongest dependence on Him—it becomes the gift.

This week, you will have the opportunity to continually ask the Lord, "What are You saying to me?" Decide now that whatever He says, you will lean into it. Obey His voice and you will know greater peace than you've ever experienced. Let the consistency of the One within you permeate you from the inside out. Though the view that surrounds you will shift, you can choose to embrace the present, knowing that His presence will always remain the same. Because Jesus remains the same, change is always an opportunity.

Flexibility, innovation, and growth are yours this week. As you embrace change, you will find that trusting God when the ground is shaky is the most worthwhile adventure of all.

DECLARE OVER YOUR WEEK:

1. Because God never changes, I will trust His faithfulness in my present moment.

2. I will embrace the freedom and joy that come with change.

3. I will value consistency over immediate rewards. God is honored by my integrity.

4. I will continually ask Jesus, "What are You saying to me?" and I will respond to that.

5. I will embrace the detours and the pivots that come up, knowing that God's best is better than I could imagine or predict.

37

Prioritize His Presence

Search for the LORD and for his
strength; continually seek him.
1 CHRONICLES 16:11 NLT

We're snappy and we're struggling. Everything feels rushed, and we know our spirit is *reacting* rather than responding. We want to stop and take time to just be with Jesus, but we feel like there's no time for it. Or we convince ourselves that once we get to a certain point or a change of season, things will shift. Isn't it interesting how we run from the very person who can actually provide the clarity, strength, and peace we're searching for?

When we're confused, why do we often wait to spend time with the One who can bring peace, perspective, and promise—especially when He's always available to us?

Every person wants healing and wholeness. And everything we do—why we relentlessly work the way we do, why we reach for things to fulfill the longing in our souls—is because we're seeking to be made whole. Our culture is famously obsessed with speed and busyness, and it can feel so tempting to give our minds away to the messages to produce more every day and night. And it's true, productivity and hustle culture can lead to a lot of things your heart longs for—promotions, status, wealth, the list goes on. But are these rhythms worth the quiet of your soul?

This week, remember you have direct access to the Maker of time. You get to extend your hands, knowing that the Giver of all good things is always at your side. You get the honor of receiving refinement from the only One who can transform hearts, knowing that every move has purpose. You get to walk in courage and boldness as you follow the Good Shepherd, knowing that uncertainty is opportunity when He is in charge.

Before you begin your day, commit to aligning your thoughts and words with His. And when you start to follow the culture's path to success? Recalibrate, receive His grace, and refresh yourself in truth. Repentance is a love letter to Him—a sacred act, not a shameful one. Knowing and trusting that the One who made you can transform any bit of brokenness into beauty is the foundation of the intimacy you were made to experience. Release the pressure to be all things to all people and reestablish rhythms that prioritize His presence in every area of your life—doing so will always protect you.

He has good things in store for you, not because of what you do but because of who you are: His treasured and beloved child.

DECLARE OVER YOUR WEEK:

1. I will make intimacy with Jesus my number one priority.

2. I will set rhythms that are healthy, realistic, and life-giving.

3. I will let the Word of God set my standard, preserve my integrity, and protect my way.

4. I will stop worrying about how I am perceived by others and focus on how I am pleasing God.

5. I will pray and believe for change, remembering that it first starts with me.

Peace Like a River

"Blessed are the peacemakers, for they
will be called children of God."
MATTHEW 5:9

I have a friend who radically confuses and inspires me on a daily basis. She asks questions that make her, and others, uncomfortable. She signs herself up for difficult conversations. She establishes boundaries with people who tell her they don't understand them. And she genuinely doesn't take shortcuts. She has shown me so much about what it means to be a peacemaker. Specifically, her willingness to fight for peace has given me a front-row seat to the healing, miracle-working power of God when we choose peace over preference, power, or pride.

If you had to sum up the life that you long for, what do you think is its foundation? Is the root of all your striving simply to have peace?

Think about the effects of water—when it enters a space, it fills every available gap, covering corners and crevices and rushing through any small crack in the walls. The power of water is often underestimated. When propelled with intensity, gathered with strength, or focused in one direction, it can move foundations. The same is true of peace; it also has a life-changing, transformative power. Like water, it is often underestimated but mighty, providing the source for everything else to remain in motion.

This week, there will be moments when you'll want to take the reins, fighting for control. Sometimes it's easy to confuse control and peace, but the two are not the same. Peace happens in the presence of one person: Jesus. Therefore, the quickest way for you to walk in peace will always be to hold His hand, sit under the shadow of His wings, and let His voice speak truth over your heart. Isn't it comforting to know that your peace is possible in every circumstance—even when you have no control—because Jesus never leaves your side?

As you enter your workplace, walk through your own front door, or step foot in a store, remember that you are a carrier of the unshakable peace of God. Because His role, reach, and reign will never change, neither will your peace, regardless of circumstances. When you start to feel anxious about a situation, combat your fears by voicing your gratitude for specific things. Find your peace by assuring yourself that God is watching, working, and making a way. Only He can calm your soul. Knowing Jesus, you get to orient yourself with a permanent posture of peace— which is the foundation of everything you do.

His heart is trustworthy, and your peace is safe. What a banner over your week!

DECLARE OVER YOUR WEEK:

1. I will be a carrier of the unshakable peace of God.

2. I will be intentional about voicing my gratitude and looking for God's hand in everything.

3. I will silence my inner critic and let God's truth wash over me. A sound mind is what He offers me.

4. I will follow the Good Shepherd as He leads me beside still waters and down paths of righteousness.

5. I will remember that obedience is linked to trust, not understanding. He is God and I am not.

The Miracle of the Mundane

Maybe it's the morning routine with God that we show up for every day. Maybe it's the diligence we give to caring for our health. Or it might be the consistent coffee dates we schedule to mentor the hearts of others. Or it could be the unseen sacrifices we make at work. It's in these everyday moments of life where true faithfulness is revealed.

Life is simply a sum of ordinary moments!

It's easy to feel like what we do daily doesn't matter in the grand scheme of things. Whether it be our attention to the house that goes unnoticed or our willingness to offer grace to those who don't seem to appreciate us, it's hard to keep showing up when we don't think our efforts are significant or seen.

But we know nothing is ordinary because we serve an extraordinary God. We know that God's economy often works opposite of the world's, so we can trust that the little things always add up to the big things, and that nothing is unseen by the One who knows everything. Because we are children of God, we get to walk with great joy and anticipation, especially in the mundane moments, knowing that our everyday lives are the perfect ground for the Miracle Maker to display His faithfulness.

This week, break free from the box that glamorizes the highs and avoids the lows. Choose to see every moment as the present gift, where God is continually surprising, saving, and sustaining you. You don't have to figure out how the small will add up to the big; when you keep your hand to the plow and your eyes on Jesus, your life will reap a harvest of righteousness that is worth far more than any gold of this world.

Just like the disciples, we get to enter into everyday life surrounded by people doing ordinary things, and we get to serve and be loved by an extraordinary God. Joy is found when we remember that the gift of life is already far from mundane or ordinary; it is the gift of unquenchable grace that can change the world.

How incredible that you get to watch God turn your natural into supernatural as you live out your week—that is nothing short of miraculous!

DECLARE OVER YOUR WEEK:

1. I will believe that small, faithful acts of obedience change the world.

2. I will offer a smile and a kind word to my own spirit first, and then to everyone else along the way.

3. I will remember that God doesn't live inside the box. His ways will always surprise, save, and sustain me.

4. I will relinquish my desire to "figure it out" and rest in the truth that God will work it out.

5. I will find deep gratitude in my everyday moments, knowing that I won't get them back.

40

Faithfulness
You Can
Trust

I t's an eerie feeling to be on the other side of a prayer
request you never expected to have," I whispered to my
husband as we sat beside our son, Sledge. We'd already
spent over five months in the hospital, and although it
was the most trying time of our lives, it was also the most
formative. Will and I frequently look at each other now
and say "hospital mindset." It's our way of reminding each
other that very few things matter, but the things that do
are worth fighting for with all you have.

Even though we know the Lord's track record, it is easy
to be consumed by the current issue, overwhelmed by the
stress in the moment, or forgetful about His character that
has carried us from moment to moment, even in the hardest seasons of our lives. What if, instead of being surprised
by our spiritual amnesia and tendency to let the created
become louder than the voice of the Creator, we chose to
build preventive measures to help us remember His heart?

The beautiful truth about our heavenly Father is that
His provision is always sufficient, His protection is always

perfect, and His priority is always His children. Our hearts are on His mind, our struggles are on His radar, and our lives are of the utmost importance to Him. The way that He cleared the path and provided fresh passion before? He will do it again. The way that He split the seas and carried us through waters we feared would consume us? He will do it again. The way that He intimately, lovingly, and gently healed our soul? He will do it again.

As you think about the situations you will encounter today and the people you'll interact with, ask Jesus to remove the scales from your eyes as you choose your thoughts, words, and actions. Let the altars of your past become ladders to your future, assuring you that the Shepherd leads you down the path only to what is good, holy, and eternal. He is weaving things together, working all for your good and His glory. Let His heart determine the countenance and posture of your heart and your hands.

Fix your eyes on His faithfulness, and you will find the fortitude for every step toward your future. God is good for His word.

DECLARE OVER YOUR WEEK:

1. I will build altars to proclaim God's faithfulness.

2. I will offer my undivided attention to Jesus first thing in the morning.

3. I will choose a heart of patience and a spirit of peace even when life feels rushed or hard.

4. I will step back and realize that the growth I prayed for often comes in the difficulties I am praying against.

5. I will remember that I always have time to pause, pray, and praise God for who He is and how He loves me.

41

The Garden
of Your Heart

Give attention to my words; incline your ear to my sayings. Do not let them depart from your eyes; keep them in the midst of your heart; for they are life to those who find them, and health to all their flesh.

PROVERBS 4:20–22 NKJV

I didn't even know it was still a thing for me. It wasn't until I experienced being left out as an adult that I realized how much I had not dealt with the wounds I experienced as a child from being excluded and bullied. But my eyes were being opened to the wound that had etched itself so deeply into the corners of my heart, I thought it belonged there.

We all have these places that feel sensitive. Often we'll avoid them until, as I was, we're forced to face them. And yet these are places the heavenly Father longs to expose so that He can help, handle, and heal. He does it so that we can live from a *whole* place.

When you come across a broken area of your heart that you know needs healing, what do you do with it? Better yet, if no one knows about it or it's possible to hide, do you still choose to bring it into the light?

Just like a garden, it is always the deep work beneath the surface that makes the fruit, the flowers, and the foliage possible. You know this, of course. But it's easy to forget when you'd rather keep anything that feels uncomfortable buried far under the surface. The truth is, the seasons of uprooting will often be the most transformative. It is usually the undoing that makes the doing purposeful; it is the healing that makes the holiness come alive.

True faith is the willingness to commit to the work beneath the surface, knowing you may look messy to others. It's easy to let your desire for comfort dictate what you're willing to dig up. If you've ever gardened, you know that some roots are far-reaching and stubborn, and it takes a lot of effort to clear the soil. But it's worth it, because only when you dig deep in the dirt to uproot decay can you make room for new life.

This week, commit to the deep work of the transformation of your soul. Recognize the places where shame or guilt have taken root, and ask for the light to break forth, letting the love of Jesus do what it was made to do—help you grow in freedom.

How do you cultivate your life like a beautiful garden? You allow honesty and space to let God handle what's beneath the surface so that you can grow in the transformation you were made to experience.

DECLARE OVER YOUR WEEK:

1. I will invite God into the deep, transformational work of my soul.

2. I will begin each day renewing my mind in truth and setting my attitude to reflect Jesus.

3. I will recognize the places where shame or guilt have seeped in and release them to Jesus.

4. I will turn to prayer in all moments.

5. I will stay present in my life instead of wishing for the circumstances of others.

42

Gentleness
Through
Words

Gentle words are a tree of life; a
deceitful tongue crushes the spirit.
PROVERBS 15:4 NLT

I sn't it funny how the healthiest and strongest relationships in our lives are usually not the easiest ones? I
think about my relationship with my husband and am
reminded that the best things often require a lot of work.
All our friends know that I joke about how honest he is, but
I really do find it incredibly refreshing. We may have different ways of arriving at a goal, but our mission is the same.
Because I know that he will fight for my best, I find peace,
strength, and so much joy from having him in my corner.

The health of our relationships really can impact our
happiness. To be in relationship with others is one of the
greatest callings of the Christian life, and few things are as
sweet as being known and cared for by the people we love.
But as we've probably experienced, lasting relationships
take a lot of work. Worthwhile relationships require intentional communication and priority in our lives. Without
great effort, relationships can easily fall into destructive
patterns or harmful habits, which are often the result of a
lack of attention and awareness.

As you go through this week, let God's presence and
His power remind you that through Him, cultivating

loving relationships with those around you is not just a possibility but a promise. Be reminded that His voice is one of a Shepherd—gentle, compassionate, and life-giving. If the advice you get, the conversations you have, or the mental chatter you hear don't align with the Shepherd's voice, let them go. Renew your mind in prayer.

Think about the relationships in your life and the opportunities you're given to be a person who extends life-giving words to others. As you approach tense moments this week, embrace compassion, offer grace, and walk in the maturity of the Holy Spirit. These are the places and people where God wants to saturate and sanctify. The coworker who tests your self-control, the child who wears down your patience, or the friend with whom you've struggled to express how you really feel—let Jesus lead you in your communication in these spaces, moment by moment. Remember that you can offer life and grace through the words you say—and those you don't.

Prioritize talking to Jesus, and you will find the endurance, patience, compassion, and joy you need to communicate with your heart and others in ways that only heaven can explain.

DECLARE OVER YOUR WEEK:

1. I will cultivate the relationships God has given me.

2. I will communicate my expectations to others instead of hoping they'll read my mind.

3. I will trust the Holy Spirit to help me discern what is true and helpful.

4. I will show up in the spaces I've been avoiding.

5. I will find my affirmation, significance, and hope in the unwavering name of Jesus.

43

Calm in the Chaos

> For God has not given us a spirit of fear, but
> of power and of love and of a sound mind.
>
> **2 TIMOTHY 1:7** NKJV

I knew that my husband was being pushed and stretched—and I could see him leaning into the Father. Despite having so much going on at work, navigating his own personal transition, and feeling the weight of leading our family in the midst of Sledge's hospitalization, I saw Will negate fear with faith. Specifically, I watched as he channeled his energy into what he could control. Worship replaced his hobbies, the hospital was his safe space for lunch, and reading with Sledge brought him deep joy. Day after day, Will was operating with a sound mind.

The phrase "sound mind" is often associated with the visual of serenity and calm. This is a nice picture but can seem impossible in a world that is often chaotic and in a culture that has a million voices vying to take the lead. As we learn about Jesus and dial into what He says about a sound mind, we will see that it is often the swirling storm around us that provides the opportunity to know divine peace. It is the presence of chaos that presents the position to stand firm on God's promises. A sound mind is not the absence of noise; it is the activation of God's voice above it all.

Consider this: If you knew that God had already equipped you with what you need to thrive, and you knew that the best is yet to come, would you walk calmly? Know that this is all true for you, exactly where you are right now. You get to choose calm amid crazy because God has empowered you to do so.

This week, you get to embrace the truth that you have the mind of Jesus Christ. This means your countenance, anticipation, and rest are based on who you trust, not on what you see—just as Jesus operated on the boat with the disciples when the storm was raging and He was sleeping. Imagine your fuel tank being replenished every morning by the One who knows exactly where you will travel today. Thank Him that your courage is not based on your own skill but on the knowledge that when you take a leap of faith or walk into the unknown, God is your safety net.

It's one thing to make plans and organize your schedule with an obligatory "have to do this" attitude. It's another to look at the week ahead and get excited about being a part of God's crew—a true fisher of people. A hopeful spirit is a powerful and often underestimated weapon against every tactic of the Enemy. Let the presence of God permeate your perspective. Reframe negative thoughts through the lens of the gospel and protect your spirit against anything that makes you second-guess your God-given authority.

Rejoice! A sound mind is His gift to you. Know that His nearness is always your calm in the crazy.

DECLARE OVER YOUR WEEK:

1. Choosing a sound mind, I will rejoice that God is trustworthy and He is near.

2. I will embrace the change that this week brings.

3. I will make plans with a positive spirit, getting excited about what is ahead and choosing to be grateful for where I am.

4. I will trust God's grace to cover me.

5. I will reframe negative thoughts with the light of truth and through the filter of eternal hope. I am in control of my mindset.

Welcoming Every New Thing

I loved living in Louisiana. I had the best friends on the planet, my small group was an amazing community, and I'd found my groove at work. Having had the opportunity to live away from my home in North Carolina, I felt like I learned so much about myself, how I operated, and what I preferred. However, God was calling me back to my home state. And while I was excited, I was also terrified and anxious. Turns out, after eight years of being away, "home" was different. My dream for Cleerely Stated began to take root, and I also got to step into the role of being an aunt. All that was *new* was richer and I was also able to benefit from the *old* relationships that I cherished.

It's humbling to reflect on the past, isn't it? Many times we realize how insistent we were on maintaining our "normal," only to realize time and again that uncertainty is the only certainty we'll ever have. Looking back, we often can't believe we were trying to stay in our comfort zone instead of trusting God with the unknown path ahead.

This week, you will face choices that don't feel like sunshine and rainbows; the difference-maker will be how you approach those circumstances. Ask God for revived passion for the place and people in front of you and proclaim that your circumstances are an opportunity, not an obligation. Choose to live with active hope that asks questions, sits with Jesus, and eagerly anticipates fresh vision and new strength. Trust the sovereignty of His will—this means that you can place your energy into what you can control and cease striving with everything else. When you cease striving, that's the opposite of becoming lazy in your faith. Instead, this is precisely when you rev up your courage, dig deep into perseverance, and proactively wait on God for the newness He is growing in your life.

Remember that with anything new, you will have an adjustment period in times of transition. Change is coming, and there will be plenty of grace for you when those moments arise. God doesn't need you to be an expert on the future you have yet to experience; He just needs you to surrender it to Him and be a willing student along the way.

Your ultimate legacy is to desire and walk in the will of God, embracing every new thing He brings and releasing all else. Are you willing?

DECLARE OVER YOUR WEEK:

1. Stepping into the new, I will receive God's grace and mercy today.

2. I will view my commitments as opportunities, not obligations.

3. I will accept that some relationships and opportunities are for a season.

4. Because God is always doing a new thing, I will continually ask for fresh vision.

5. I will walk with confidence and humility, both rooted in the absolute sovereignty of my Creator.

Safe, Secure, and Sure of It

I magine feeling the wind in your hair as you soar through the sky and see the land from a different view. You experience unbridled freedom, and joy fills your soul as you experience a thrill like you've never known. Then, zip-lining through the mountain clearing and reaching the other side, you feel relief as your feet ground themselves once again on the earth.

How comforting is it to know that no matter what, we have a safe place to fall? How helpful is it to know that when we walk forward in courage, God honors and meets us there?

There is something that every human heart, no matter how hard or how bruised or broken, was made to crave: safety. We were crafted with the yearning to know that we belong and that our belonging is not in jeopardy. The hard part about this truth is not the desire for safety—that's a blessing! The difficult thing is how often we will feel tempted to find our security in places and people other than Jesus, and in roles other than being a child of the King.

Think about how you feel when your safety is threatened in any area: your fear rises, your anxiety pings, and your emotions begin to consume you, convincing you that you need to wrestle for control. But Jesus has already given you the greatest reminder and surest revelation you could ever have: He is your safe refuge in every circumstance, especially the ones that feel shaky.

This week, you don't have to walk on eggshells, wondering if you'll be accepted or liked. You get to enter situations with a posture of peace, a temperament of tenderness, and a disposition of delight because you know who is for you and with you. Knowing your security allows you to be proactive in walking with gratitude and celebration. So be intentional about voicing God's goodness and decide now how you will walk throughout the week, certain that your joy is not in jeopardy and your security is sure.

Remember that the One who is holding you desires abundance, purpose, and strength for your life far more than you do. Trust that His plan for your fulfillment is greater than anything you could wrangle up and stabilize yourself with His promises—His true, life-giving, and hope-filled promises.

Be courageous with your steps, bold with your prayers, and open with your resources. Rest in the truth that nothing, nowhere, and no one is as safe, secure, and steadfast as the Shepherd who's holding you.

DECLARE OVER YOUR WEEK:

1. I will find my stability and strength, my sure foundation, in the sovereignty of God.

2. I will decide my emotional temperament before I enter every situation.

3. I will laugh often, celebrate daily, and establish traditions of gratitude to ground me.

4. I will remember that my belonging is never in jeopardy because I am a child of the King.

5. I will sleep peacefully because the Good Shepherd holds my tomorrow.

46

The Ripple
Effect

I remember watching an old coworker of mine as she operated in the office. Her attentiveness to detail heightened everyone else's preparedness. Her desire for excellence pushed everyone to go the extra mile. And her willingness to get her own hands dirty challenged everyone to walk in the same humility. During our Christmas slow-cooker challenge, when everyone was getting superlatives, she was voted "Most Influential Work Ethic." She was utterly shocked, which made her win that much greater! Her leadership was woven into the fabric of her being, which made her influence one that truly changed the atmosphere of the company.

Do you ever hear the word *leader* and convince yourself you are not in that group? Or maybe your leadership qualities are reserved for a particular area of life or a season you will reach "down the road" once you master some skill, rhythm, or practice?

Whatever you're doing, wherever you're reading this, however you got here, and whatever your path has looked like thus far, one thing rings true: you are called to be a leader right where you are. Being a leader is not an elite calling reserved for those who have a higher status. Being a leader is your God-given right and responsibility as a child of the living, true, and unchanging God. Because you know the Waymaker, you are a culture shaper, not a culture follower. You will have many opportunities in which you get to answer this question: "Will I conform to those around me, or will I stand firm and remain set apart?"

This week, choose to be the leader He has called you to be. When you feel discouraged or drained, plug into the Source. Pray. Read. Get still with the Lord. Leaders still have hard emotions; they just know where to take them and how to see if they align with truth. Your emotions are helpful indicators, reminding you that you can't make it on your own. But don't forget: you have constant access to the Holy Spirit. His unlimited supply of kindness, self-control, and love will provide all that you need to be a leader in how you respond to others. As the Holy Spirit whispers gentleness to your soul, extend that warmth to others, aware that everyone is fighting battles you know nothing about.

Armor up and lead others in the way of Jesus. Surrender the performance mentality and harness the praise mentality instead. God is strong in you.

DECLARE OVER YOUR WEEK:

1. Because God calls me a leader, I will seek to be a culture shaper rather than a culture follower.

2. I will sit with Jesus first and foremost, reminding my heart that He is for me and with me.

3. I will put on the armor of God every day and remind my heart that I already stand in victory.

4. I will lean on the endurance and peace of the Holy Spirit when I feel drained or discouraged.

5. I will always extend kindness, remembering that many are fighting battles I know nothing about.

47

Embracing the Journey

H ave you ever seen one of those videos that shows an
athlete sprinting to accidentally—but earnestly!—
score in the opponent's goal? Despite their passion
and desire to win, their efforts are misaligned. Those who
are running after perfection can learn from this lesson.
Their zest may be strong, and they may even be capable,
but they're running toward a goal that actually sets them
backward. But *releasing* perfectionism allows us to make
realistic progress in the present.

What do you resonate more with: desiring perfection
or embracing the journey?

You are not alone if you leaned more toward the first
option. It's human nature to desire perfection, even when
we know it's an impossible standard. The hard part about
letting go of this mentality is embracing the surrender
and dependence that doing so requires. When you really
want to get to the other side of a hard situation, experience the power of a breakthrough, or walk in the blessings
of the harvest ahead, it's easy to get tunnel vision of the
finish line. If we're not careful, we automatically put on

blinders to the beauty that surrounds us as we make our way there.

The truth is, refinement is often painful and hard. As God chips away at the old, change is required. Refinement is also God's love letter back to us—the ability to receive the sanctification of the perfect Savior and grow in righteousness is such an incredible gift. The meaning of life is not found in carrying out the romantic ideal we once had in our heads. Rather, it is discovered as we embrace the reality before us—the messy, often entangled, and beautifully sanctifying life.

This week, welcome whatever pruning your heavenly Father brings, no matter how hard or how heavy it may feel in the moment. Remember that the process of pruning is exactly that—a process, which proves it is not immediate and it is also temporary. Recognize divine opportunities—moments that prompt your courage and invite your trust are mercy in disguise. Open your eyes to the people around you and focus more on being interested in them than proving you are interesting. This curiosity will help you have a heart of understanding and a spirit of acceptance. Release the fixation on the outcome or the destination and embrace every part of the process. This is faith: the journey of becoming more like Jesus.

Take heart—breakthrough is ahead, His strength will sustain you, and wisdom is being sown into the roots of your soul. This is good ground.

DECLARE OVER YOUR WEEK:

1. I will constantly remind myself that growth is a process and the journey is the reward.

2. Every morning, I will remind my soul that God has my best in mind and He has my day.

3. I will welcome whatever pruning God brings, knowing that the results of refinement are faith, strength, and peace.

4. I will recognize divine opportunities.

5. I will praise God for the breakthrough and progress that are ahead.

48

Humility
Brings
Wisdom

Humility is the fear of the LORD; its wages
are riches and honor and life.

PROVERBS 22:4

One of my mentors is, literally, a genius. She would certainly never tell you that. But her resourcefulness, vocabulary, ability to recall, and her ability to problem-solve blow me away. And yet I distinctly remember her talking to several women half her age, asking them a million questions, certain that she had something to glean from them. Her eagerness to remain a student and her desire to learn from others allow God to use her in mighty ways.

Humility is a foundational attribute required for so many Christlike qualities. Think about it: If we want to be gentle, we must humble ourselves so the whisper of God can speak through us. If we want to be compassionate, we must take the time to stop, see, and sit with others, giving space for them to tell their story. If we want to respond with wisdom, we must let go of our pride, surrender our perceptions, and let the perspective of heaven lead us. It is humility that brings awareness and space for the Spirit to have His way in us.

This week, there will be moments when you'll want to self-protect, thinking you have to prove your point in order to succeed. In these moments, pause and get with Jesus. Remind your heart that He is your Protector, and humility is your greatest weapon. God's economy and theology are often the opposite of the world's. Your willingness to let go of your own agenda and surrender to your heavenly Father's will reap the greatest rewards, both on this earth and in eternity.

Growth is exciting, alluring, and impressive, but it is far more dangerous to nurture a garden that's growing the wrong things. Survey what is growing and take inventory of what you have been watering—do those things please the Lord? Humble yourself at the feet of Jesus and communicate with Him about what feels worthy of your pursuit. It will always be your attention to His will and the implementation of your humility that preserve your life and lead you down the path of righteousness.

As you lean into His direction and care for you, you will find more strength to be obedient and experience the peace that comes from yearning to do His will. Remember that humility is driven by love, not shame or guilt. As you understand your need for grace, love and awe will be your response. A life grounded in humility results in an eternal posture of worship.

It is not how high you can jump that determines your ability. Rather, it is often how long you're willing to stay flexible that proves your strength.

DECLARE OVER YOUR WEEK:

1. I will practice humility.

2. I will begin my day telling Jesus everything that's on my mind and letting Him help me.

3. I will be the kind of friend I pray to have.

4. I will take inventory of what's growing in the garden of my life and constantly ask, "Does this honor God and point to heaven?"

5. I will surrender to the will of the Father in all moments.

49

A Timeline You Can Trust

> But do not forget this one thing, dear friends:
> With the Lord a day is like a thousand years, and a
> thousand years are like a day. The Lord is not slow in
> keeping his promise, as some understand slowness.
> Instead he is patient with you, not wanting anyone
> to perish, but everyone to come to repentance.
>
> **2 PETER 3:8-9**

How come it's working out for everyone else, but not for me?" I knew my friend felt slighted and frustrated. This precious young woman, who has willingly and happily cheered on every bride in our friend group, finally let me hear her own frustration. As she wept, she asked me if there was anything wrong with her. My words fell flat as I also questioned why the Lord would withhold something good from someone who has so kindly shown up for His people.

When something doesn't go as planned, when the results don't come when we thought they would, or when our prayers have yet to be answered, do we get frustrated by God's timeline? Do we feel tempted to run ahead or somehow trigger a different sequence of events?

Our timeline is usually based on what we can see— the past that's led us here, the work we're doing in the current season, and our dreams and hopes for the future.

Many of those prayers are etched into the fiber of our being—maybe that includes owning a business, becoming a parent, pursuing a health goal, or mastering a skill that's been hard for us. But sometimes other desires slip in subconsciously, often birthed from the curated pictures we see of the lives around us, the pressure we feel from the world, or the unrealistic standards of perfection we set for ourselves. This tension between dreaming big but not putting our happiness in the outcome of our dreams is the place where faith is tested, built, and refined.

This week, when you find yourself sizing up your life or feeling stagnant in your growth, go to the Maker of time and ask Him, "Father, will You remind me that with You, I lack no good thing?" Your acquisition of things won't bring contentment this week. You'll find peace when you abide in Jesus and remember that His plans for you are good and His provision for you is trustworthy.

When you walk in step with the Spirit, you are always right on time and in the right place. Take a walk and let nature assure you that God is big enough to cover your gaps, catalyze your creativity, and create the most beautiful canvases out of the most unexpected color palettes.

Step-by-step, moment by moment, the Holy Spirit is taking you exactly where you need to go.

DECLARE OVER YOUR WEEK:

1. Trusting in God's timing, I will release the fear of falling behind or getting left out.

2. I will remember that change brings renewal, beauty, growth, and hope.

3. I will walk with Jesus.

4. I will schedule time to celebrate the small wins.

5. I will praise God for His timeline and how He uses the unexpected to challenge and encourage my perseverance.

50

A Quiet Life

"Be still, and know that I am God; I will be exalted
among the nations, I will be exalted in the earth."

PSALM 46:10

We see the laundry that needs to be folded. We pass by the dishes that need to be put in the dishwasher. We quiet our brain that's buzzing with the day's details. Instead of being bullied by these demands, we choose to sit down with Jesus first. We're convinced that His presence is the key ingredient to being productive in the spaces that truly matter. Through stillness, we receive the strength, sustenance, and sound mind we need to be effective wherever we are.

As a culture, there is a high value placed on productivity and busyness. This ever-growing trend, accelerated by social media and the digital world, tends to convince us that a purposeful life is founded in a productive life—the kind of productivity that often means we have to sacrifice our priorities in order to meet deadlines and impress others.

However, the Shepherd has a different way of operating that, while seeming counterproductive, proves to be the way to the life we're craving. The only way to become aware of all that God is doing is to take the time to stop, be still, and soak in the blessings around us. It is through quieting our soul that we find the space to listen to His voice, heed His direction, and receive His adoration.

This week, don't fall prey to the temptation to be everywhere and do everything; this pressure is always a setup for burnout and discouragement. Instead, place the highest value on living a quiet life where your first priority and greatest delight is spending time with the One who made you. Fill your mind with truth as you dig deep into His Word, and let Scripture help you find your deep breath again.

Taking the time to be still may feel stagnant, but trust that God will honor that time, order your steps, and renew your energy for the day ahead. Recognize the boundary lines He has drawn for you and be diligent within them. These boundaries help you keep Him first, call your attention to the flock He has assigned to you, and keep your focus on expanding heaven rather than impressing the world. As you commune with Jesus, you will find the patience, perseverance, and power to show up where God has called you this week.

Stillness is the posture that provides purpose for your movements. Linger with Jesus.

DECLARE OVER YOUR WEEK:

1. I will prioritize stillness with my Creator before all else.

2. I will fill my mind with truth and fortify my heart with hope planted in the promises of God.

3. I will tend to my own garden with diligence and gratitude.

4. I will recognize when my patience is low and let this call me back to solitude.

5. I will place high value on a quiet life, rooted in confidence in Jesus and focused on the cross He bore for me.

Rhythms of a Grace-Filled Life

Above all else, guard your heart, for
everything you do flows from it.

PROVERBS 4:23

M y friend's marching orders were very specific: lots of water throughout the day, dinner by 7:00 p.m., and no phone after 8:00 p.m. These were all necessary boundaries in order to begin her new routine. My friend had experienced a deep trauma, and her response? "If I'm going to handle healing well, I have got to change my routines." It was crazy to see how much modifying her nightly routine transformed her morning schedule, which in turn prompted her new exercise habit, which fueled her nutrition challenge, and later changed her approach to her entire workday. When she put healthy boundaries in place, she thrived.

The same goes for our lives and specifically our hearts—the most honorable of intentions cannot protect us if the needed borders aren't established. The truth is, most long-lasting transformation happens one step at a time. Repetitive attention heightens our aptitude, catalyzes courage to keep showing up, and builds our trust.

This week, you don't have to become frantic over all that must be done; instead, commit to doing the next right thing (literally, just the next thing) on the current path God has called you to. As you operate with diligence, excellence, and wisdom right where you are, you will find the strength you need for where you are going. When God calls you to set a new boundary to protect your soul, do so with confidence that His lot for you is secure and significant.

When it feels hard to set the boundary or you fear what you will lose if you do, talk to your heavenly Father about it. Ask Him to remind you of His nearness and His faithfulness in every gift that He gives and takes away.

When the pressure surrounding you gets the best of you, and you fail, don't worry. There's a reason why your loving Father gave you many scriptures about releasing shame, embracing grace, trusting His plan, and trying again. An active faith is not the presence of perfect boundary lines and discernment; it is the willingness to be wrong, receive God's instruction, and reset your life accordingly.

How do you know what is for you and what is not? Read His Word. Certainly, there will be a difference in your days that begin with the Word; even when the circumstances aren't ideal, being rooted in His promises will help you find newfound strength grounded in the things you can't see on the surface.

Time is a gift. Attend to what matters, cultivate healthy thought patterns, and trust the boundary lines God has drawn for you.

DECLARE OVER YOUR WEEK:

1. I will walk with the confidence that I can establish healthy boundaries.

2. I will begin my day with the Word of God.

3. I will pray specifically and intentionally for my relationships—that I would learn to speak life into them and not try to control them.

4. I will do one thing at a time, not letting my mind become frantic over all that must be done.

5. Remembering that time is a gift, I will stay in the present and trust God's promises in every process.

52

Redirect, Renew, and Refresh

> "Look at the birds of the air; they do not sow or reap or store away in barns, and yet your heavenly Father feeds them. Are you not much more valuable than they? Can any one of you by worrying add a single hour to your life?"
>
> **MATTHEW 6:26-27**

When people are upset with me, it makes my whole body want to turn inside out. Recently, I was navigating a miscommunication with a family member, and I felt like my mind was on a treadmill at max speed, and I couldn't find the emergency stop. As I let my mind calm down and took a step back, I realized I had taken false responsibility for feelings and interpretations I had no control over. Slowly but surely, I recalibrated, reset myself with Jesus, and was reminded that peace really is a decision to trust Him.

The human mind is powerful—it was made to be. The Lord wired our brains to form thought patterns, make connections, and create exciting, imaginative scenarios. The problem is not our mind, our imagination, or our tendency to go rogue on the intended route. The issue is the thoughts that don't align with truth, the ones that creep in ever so slowly that we start to believe. These little white lies the Enemy likes to plant in our mind are like termites, eating away from within and causing destruction before we ever realize there is an infestation.

Here is a novel idea for the hamster wheel: disrupt it. When you sense those destructive thoughts starting to form, when you feel social media triggering a web of lies about your identity, when you find yourself making snap judgments about friends' comments, when your anxious brain is reaching far into the uncertainty of the future—choose to stop it. When a what-if question comes to the surface, redirect and rephrase your thought with this: *I can't wait to see how God shows up here.* Even when your feelings seem far from celebratory, speak what is true, holy, and possible with Jesus. It's not "faking it" to speak faith out loud when your reality feels far from it. It is wise and holy to remind your heart of God's character when your body seems to have forgotten it.

This week, plan for rest to be your daily companion. Regardless of what's on your to-do list, you get to operate knowing your life is not a performance—it is an act of worship. The pressure is off. Because the Holy Spirit is the Person of peace and He is within you, peace is yours everywhere you go.

You are set apart, and your mind is a powerful tool for building God's kingdom. Believe it because it's true!

DECLARE OVER YOUR WEEK:

1. I will disrupt anxious thoughts with God's Word—reading it, speaking it, and claiming it. God has me.

2. I will embrace that heaven's pace and priorities are much different from the world's.

3. I will simplify anything I can so I can focus on what is true, necessary, and timely for right now.

4. I will replace my restless "What if?" questions with proclamations of "I can't wait to see how God..."

5. I will plan for fun, rest, and peace to be my daily companions.

About the
Author

Cleere Cherry Reaves is the owner and creator of Cleerely Stated, a successful online boutique whose inspirational products can be found in retail stores all over the United States. She is also the host of the growing *Let's Be Cleere* podcast. Known for her relatable writing style, Cleere's mission is to help others see themselves and the world around them through the eyes of Jesus. Cleere and her husband, Will, live in Greenville, North Carolina, and welcomed their first child, son Sledge, into the world in the summer of 2021.